HE GAVE US SO MUCH

ROBERT CARDINAL SARAH

He Gave Us So Much

A Tribute to Benedict XVI

Translated by Michael J. Miller

IGNATIUS PRESS   SAN FRANCISCO

Original French edition:
Il nous a tant donné
© 2023 by Librairie Arthème Fayard, Paris, France

Cover photo © Stefano Spaziani

Cover design by Nuit de Chine (France)

© 2023 by Ignatius Press, San Francisco
All rights reserved
ISBN 978-1-62164-684-6 (HB)
ISBN 978-1-64229-301-2 (eBook)
Library of Congress Control Number 2023941626
Printed in the United States of America ∞

*To Pope Francis, in thanks
for his merciful fatherhood
over the whole Church*

CONTENTS

INTRODUCTION

Why another book about Benedict XVI? For me it is out of the question that I should settle scores in it or lower myself to the petty game of revelations concerning the history of a man whose words and deeds have been so decisive for the history of the Church.

Do not expect an academic synthesis of his theological teaching, either. Do not look for an anthology of his great speeches to the world. You will find neither the conferences in Subiaco nor the speech in the Collège des Bernardins in Paris nor the one in the Bundestag in Berlin. I leave all that in the hands of the professional theologians. I am also certain that many researchers will dedicate their efforts to scrutinizing the immense work of Joseph Ratzinger.

My purpose in writing this book was to reveal the power of his teaching, for Benedict XVI was a spiritual master. I think that his very precise and profound theological thought is rooted in an authentic mystical and spiritual experience. Therefore, you will find in this book a general idea of the soul of Joseph Ratzinger. I tried to recall the times when, furtively, he opened up the secret recesses of his heart.

These moments outline an original path to God. They compose the portrait of a saint. They invite us to follow him. To this I added various texts that I had published over the years. I revised, expanded, and updated them. In them you may discover an unexpected, unknown Benedict XVI. In them you perceive the coherence of the

9

immense treasure that he left to us. You sense that his teaching and his example are a continent, still unexplored, where the Church will be able to find nourishment for a long time.

Finally, I wished to offer to the reader several texts by Benedict XVI that accompany him on an itinerary, for he was and remains a shepherd of souls. In many cases, these are forgotten, little-known texts that invite us to set out with him on a path toward God.

How can this itinerary be summed up? It would not be possible to understand its unity and coherence without emphasizing its first and sole preoccupation: God. Ultimately, Joseph Ratzinger would never stop returning to it. He would never give up contemplating God himself. This first look at God is what explains his incessant warnings: forgetfulness of God threatens the world with a moral, anthropological, and political catastrophe. Only faith can save reason, society, and personal freedom from shipwreck. The rejection of God engenders the denial of the most fundamental human realities. In this sense, Joseph Ratzinger would draw the most profound conclusions from the suffering inflicted on him by his experience of the Hitler regime.

In his fatherly concern, Benedict XVI took to heart the missionary duty to discuss wisely, rigorously, and with an acute sense of accuracy a question of capital importance: Who is God? He had the habit of repeating in his private conversations: "There are many important subjects, but the most important is faith in God." This is the center around which his preaching, his papacy, and his papal ministry revolved. Others may act differently, but the main purpose of the pope is precisely this: God. Certainly, it is difficult to speak seriously about God, François Varillon says. Even so, it is necessary to do it.

Am I not under the obligation to talk seriously about God to myself? Talking to God implies talking about God, even in the privacy of the self. Otherwise, I run the risk of slipping unconsciously into adoration of a hybrid divinity, a bit pagan, a bit Jewish, a bit Christian. As a priest I do not want to withhold from my brothers this talk to God and about God which is the root of my consecrated life [as a steward of the mysteries of God]. Should it happen that, having to talk about God, I wish to touch upon other matters—changing the world, social justice, [peace in the world, welcoming migrants, intercultural or interreligious dialogue, protecting the environment], economic or political revolution [or reform]—I must first make sure that I am not escaping from my own depth. The depth of others can only be reached through one's own depth. If I am tempted to cease speaking about God to others, it may be that I have stopped talking about him to myself.[1]

Maybe it is because God is no longer at the center of my life and my preoccupations. How bitter it is to notice that almost nowhere around me is there an opportunity to pay a little attention to God and to show interest in God!

All the rest of his teaching must be read in this light. Think of the decisive place that he assigned to the liturgy, the privileged place of meeting with God, for the future of the Church.

Very early, after Vatican Council II, Benedict XVI expressed this concern. When he saw that the worship of the Church was entering a profound crisis, he immediately sounded the alarm and dared to write that, contrary to the original nature of the liturgical movement,

[1] François Varillon, *The Humility and Suffering of God*, trans. Nellie Marans (New York: Alba House, 1983), 6–7. Bracketed material does not appear in the English translation. The French edition indicates that the words within the third pair of brackets were added by the author.

the liturgical reform, in its concrete realization, has moved
ever farther away from this origin. The result has not been
a revival but a devastation. On the one hand, we have a
liturgy that has degenerated into a show, in which people
try to make religion interesting by means of fashionable
nonsense and enticing moral maxims, with momentary
success in the group of liturgical fabricators, and an attitude of retreat all the more pronounced among those
who seek in the liturgy not a spiritual showmaster, but an
encounter with the living God before whom all "doing"
becomes insignificant; for only this encounter can make us
reach the true riches of being.[2]

Joseph Ratzinger wanted to lead us to rediscover the
greatness, the sacredness, and the divine origin of the liturgy so as to put us face to face with God. From the beginning of his reflection, meditating on the Book of Exodus
in *The Spirit of the Liturgy*, he affirms that the liturgy is
in the divine order, that it derives its standard [*mesure*]
and its organization [*ordonnance*] from God himself and
from his revelation. Indeed, the objective of the Book of
Exodus is to lead the people to adoration in the liturgical
form determined by God himself. God gives the order to
Pharaoh: "Let my people go, so that they may serve me
in the wilderness" (Ex 7:16). And so Israel sets out on a
journey, not to become a nation like the others, but to
serve and adore God. The Promised Land is given so as
to become a place in which to adore the True God. Mere
possession of the land, simple national autonomy would

<hr>

[2] Joseph Ratzinger, preface to *La Réforme liturgique en question*, by Klaus
Gamber (Le Barroux, France: Sainte-Madeleine, 1992) (French edition). The
preface was translated into English by Peter Kwasniewski for *New Liturgical
Movement*, https://www.newliturgicalmovement.org/2023/02/translation-of
-ratzingers-preface-to.html#.ZDW-WubMldU.

lower Israel to the rank of all other peoples.[3] And so God shows Israel how to adore him and what to offer him. Man is not the one who fabricates his liturgy as he pleases like a simple game. The liturgy is not fabricated any more than one can fabricate a living being or something that is alive. It is received; it is given. The liturgy cannot spring from our imagination or be the product of our creativity; then it would only be an aimless cry or a mere affirmation of self. The worship of the golden calf, which had been fabricated by the priest Aaron and the people of Israel (Ex 32; Deut 9:7—10:5), illustrates this self-celebration of the community that thinks that it is all-powerful and therefore capable of fashioning its worship and liturgy for itself. At this stage, the liturgy is nothing but an empty game. Worse yet, it is apostasy, the tragic abandonment of God under the cloak of the sacred.

Farther on, addressing the question of rite in the Church, in other words, the concrete arrangements made by the Church to achieve authentic worship, Joseph Ratzinger clearly emphasizes that in the expression of these rites the individual discovers a world that he himself does not produce; he enters into a reality greater than he, over which he has no control since, ultimately, it came from a revelation.

This is why Eastern Christians highlight the inviolable character of the liturgy by using the expression "Divine Liturgy" to designate it. As for the Western Church, it always had a stronger sense of the historical element, a tendency that Jungmann sums up in this lapidary formula: "the liturgy that has come to be", thereby indicating that this becoming continues in a process of organic growth and is not the product of willed actions. In other words

---

[3] Joseph Ratzinger, *The Spirit of the Liturgy*, commemorative ed., trans. John Saward (San Francisco: Ignatius Press, 2018), 29–31.

one cannot compare the liturgy to a device that one fabricates, a mechanism that can be taken apart and repaired
at will. Rather, it should be compared to a plant, to a
growing organism with internal laws that determine the
modalities of its future development. In this sense, all
liturgical reform must be thought of as an organic development of a divine gift. The Constitution *Sacrosanctum
concilium* recalled this in clear, imperious terms. Benedict
was vividly aware of this, and his liturgical work as pope
has here its most radical explanation:

> Eventually, the idea of the givenness of the liturgy, the
> fact that one cannot do with it what one will, faded from
> the public consciousness of the West. In fact, the First
> Vatican Council had in no way defined the pope as an
> absolute monarch. On the contrary, it presented him as
> the guarantor of obedience to the revealed Word. The
> pope's authority is bound to the tradition of faith, and that
> also applies to the liturgy. It is not "manufactured" by the
> authorities. Even the pope can only be a humble servant of
> its lawful development and abiding integrity and identity.[4]

We cannot thank Benedict XVI enough for having
helped us in this way to penetrate into the mystery and the
grandeur of the divine liturgy in which we really encounter God. The liturgy must first show Jesus Christ, present
in the liturgical actions, "the same [One] now offering,
through the ministry of priests, who formerly offered himself on the cross" (*SC*, no. 7). The liturgy is not liturgy
unless it allows Christ Jesus in his transfiguring presence to
shine through the signs, the gestures, the sacred words that
the Church has handed down to us in her rites.

[4] Ibid., 179–80.

Let us ask God that we might become children like
Benedict. That is how he lived the sacred liturgy that prepared him for the true liturgy in the next world. For, he
says to us again,

> Liturgy [is] a reminder that we are all children, or should
> be children, in relation to that true life toward which we
> yearn to go. Liturgy [is] a kind of anticipation, a rehearsal,
> a prelude for the life to come, for eternal life, which Saint
> Augustine describes, by contrast with life in this world, as
> a fabric woven, no longer of exigency and need, but of the
> freedom of generosity and gift. Seen thus, liturgy would
> be the rediscovery within us of true childhood, of open-
> ness to a greatness still to come, which is still unfulfilled
> in adult life. Here, then, would be the concrete form of
> hope, which lives in advance the life to come, the only
> true life, which initiates us into authentic life—the life of
> freedom, of intimate union with God, of pure openness
> to our fellowman.[5]

Recall also the particular attention that he paid to monasteries and to contemplative prayer. He regarded it as a
decisive matter for the whole Church that in some places
the effective primacy of God should be manifested and
concretely implemented by chanting the Divine Office,
silent prayer, meditation on Scripture, and the deployment
of a solemn liturgy to which nothing should be preferred.

Again, his sense of God was the basis for his uncondi-
tional love for the Word of God, handed down by tradition and Sacred Scripture and proposed to everyone
reliably by the inviolable Magisterium of the Church.

Finally, his love for God prompted him to love and
to guide the priests who are responsible for proclaiming

[5] Ibid., 28.

God's presence in the world. He loved the priesthood as a gift from God to humanity.

When I look at the life of Benedict XVI, a verse from the Gospel stands out in my mind: "Learn from me; for I am gentle and lowly in heart" (Mt 11:29). Through his whole life, which was rooted in God, through his teaching, which was drawn from prayer and contemplation, he would be this reflection of the gentle, lowly heart of Christ.

May Benedict XVI, a spiritual teacher, pastor of hearts, and father of souls, guide us and protect the Church.

Part One

Mystical Portrait of Benedict XVI

"He will remain the father
of our souls for a long time"

PROLOGUE

God Is!

Confronting the immensity of the work of Benedict XVI makes a person dizzy. For thirty years, at the side of Saint John Paul II, then as his successor on the throne of Peter, he laid the spiritual and theological foundations of the Church of the third millennium. What, then, is the key to this cathedral of the thought of Joseph Ratzinger? Rather than a quality, rather than a psychological feature, the architectonic principle of the work of Pope Benedict is in God—more precisely, it is God himself, contemplated and loved.

As he wrote as early as 1977: "The fundamental orientation of Christian conversion is: 'God is.'" Through these very sober words, the light of faith rises to the surface. "God exists, and, consequently, the 'gods' are not God. Accordingly, we must worship him, no one else." Joseph Ratzinger does not base his teaching on a personal experience or on a subjective feeling or a particular history, but on a fact that is essential to him: God *is*. You have to read this meditation from the 1970s in which the future pope punctuates [*scande*] his talk with this exclamation that is at the same time contemplative and jubilant: *God is!* The very depths of the soul of Joseph Ratzinger are revealed in it: "God is—[which means,] therefore, that which is true and right is superior to all our goals and interests. That which is worthless in earthly terms has a worth. The adoration of God himself, true adoration, exists, protecting man from the dictatorship of goals. Only this adoration is able to protect him from the dictatorship of idols."[1]

God *is*! How liberating! At an hour when the Church seems to be obsessed with herself, with her structures, with her future, her concern about adapting to the Western world, Benedict XVI tells us: at the foundation of everything, there are these wondrous, loving words: *God is*. At an hour when people waste so much time in meetings, in a national synodal way (the sole subject of which is us, ourselves, and we), he invites us to turn our attention away from ourselves so as to turn to God, this God whose being is the sole light.

Allow me to dream: Benedict XVI would certainly have loved to convoke a synod, the sole subject of which would have been: *God is!*

But I would like to caution my readers to make no mistake. This exclamation, this "*God is*", must not be understood as a cold, rigid conceptual conclusion. It seems to me personally that I hear these words as though Benedict XVI pronounced them aloud in front of me. I seem to hear them uttered by his gentle voice, trembling with emotion before the mystery, his voice entirely in love with the reality being contemplated. *God is* does not just mean God exists, but rather, in the intensive sense, God *is* in fullness, he displays the whole infinite breadth of his being. In affirming this "*God is*", Joseph Ratzinger affirms in the same statement the certainty of being loved by God:

> God is—and this also means that all of us are his creatures.... We are creatures whom he has willed and whom he has destined for eternity.... Man is not the product of chance.... Man owes his origin to God's creative love.

[1]Joseph Ratzinger, *The God of Jesus Christ: Meditations on the Triune God*, trans. Brian McNeil (San Francisco: Ignatius Press, 2008), 28.

God is—and here we must underline that little word *is*. For God truly is: in other words, he is at work, he acts.... He has not abdicated in favor of his world-machine; he has not lost his own function in a world where everything would function autonomously without him. No, the world is and remains *his* world. He can act, and he does act in a very real way now, in this world and in our life.[2]

Here the beautiful soul of Joseph Ratzinger is revealed. He has been seized by the love of God and has let himself be seized. This "*God is*" encapsulates the whole theological and, I dare say, mystical experience of Benedict XVI. He experienced to the very depths of his being God's love for him, God's goodness, God's mercy.

[2] Ibid.

I

Entering into the Mystery of the Son to Contemplate the Father

I am personally struck by the experience that Benedict XVI had of the divine fatherhood. It seems to me that Joseph Ratzinger mystically entered into the experience of the divine filiation through his union with the Incarnate Son, Jesus. This statement may be surprising. However, he left us words of surpassing spiritual power: "Without Jesus, we do not know what 'Father' truly is. This becomes visible in his prayer, which is the foundation of his being.... Prayer was the center out of which he lived.... Jesus shows us what it means to lead the whole of one's life on the basis of the affirmation that 'God is.' "[1] I think that Joseph Ratzinger immersed himself in the filial prayer of Jesus, that he let himself be shaped by it so as to discover the profound and mysterious reality of the divine fatherhood. For him, to say "Our Father" is not a formula, but a reality that is experienced.

> How, then, do we know that fatherhood is a kindness on which we can rely and that God, despite all outward appearances, is not playing with the world, but loves it dependably? For this, it was necessary that God should

---

[1]Joseph Ratzinger, *The God of Jesus Christ: Meditations on the Triune God*, trans. Brian McNeil (San Francisco: Ignatius Press, 2008), 33–34.

show himself, overthrow the images, and set up a new criterion. This takes place in the Son, in Christ. In his prayer,
he plunges the totality of his life into the abyss of truth and
of goodness that is God. It is only on the basis of this Son
that we truly experience what God is.[2]

These words of Benedict XVI sketch his portrait:
Through the intervention of prayer, "he plunge[d] the
totality of his life into the abyss of truth and of goodness
that is God." He identified with Jesus, the Son of the
Father. Everyone remembers the day when, meditating
aloud before the Blessed Sacrament in Lourdes, he partly
revealed the secret of his most intimate prayer: "Lord, take
us into your love, the infinite love that is eternally the love
of the Father for the Son." That evening, a ray from his
soul illumined the grotto of Massabielle.

The virtues of spiritual childhood

Benedict XVI entered into the mystery of the divine
childhood, of God who had become a child. He loved
to meditate on this mystery of the face of Christ. "The
Church received the mission to show everyone this loving
face of God, manifest in Jesus Christ", he proclaimed in
Lourdes in 2008. Contemplation of the face of the Incarnate Word characterized his soul and his whole person.
It is quite striking to observe the photographs of Joseph
Ratzinger. Shortly after his elevation to the throne of
Peter, his face mellowed. We saw a childlike smile appear
on it. During his audiences and celebrations, the cameras
sometimes focused on this face. I was struck then by the

[2] Ibid., 33.

joyful innocence and lucidity that emerged from it. The mystery of childhood left its mark even on the features of Benedict XVI.

Someone said about him that he had the piety of a first communicant. It seems to me that this remark is much more than a psychological description. It tells of the path of his soul, which radiated the virtues of childhood. Like a child in the arms of his father, he was radiant with a quiet peace.

Prince of peace

"Christ is our true peace: in him, by his Cross, God has reconciled the world to Himself." When we discover these words, which were pronounced on January 1, 2012, we cannot help thinking of Saint Augustine's definition: peace is the tranquility of order. Joseph Ratzinger lived out this radical peace, this security of a man who is in his place as a child of God. This sure, strong peace is only the radiance of a form of truth that characterized his whole personality. In him there was no shadow of a lie, of an attempt to seduce, of political or tactical dissimulation. On the contrary, in Benedict XVI everything was perfectly transparent. Because he *was* in the truth of his being with regard to God, he was fully true with regard to other people.

Once again, Benedict XVI followed the example of Christ: "[Jesus] has disclosed the full truth about humanity and about human history. The power of his grace makes it possible to live 'in' and 'by' truth, since he alone is completely true and faithful. Jesus is the truth that gives us peace."[3] We can gauge the extent to which truth, for

---

[3] Message for the World Day of Peace (January 1, 2006).

Benedict XVI, is not just a concept. It is an attitude of the soul. Conforming to the truth amounts to being fully human by adhering to Christ, who is the divine Truth.

The "tranquility" of Benedict XVI is this peace of a man who has entered wholly into the divine Order. This truth of his existence conferred on him a sense of security, a peaceful and contagious strength, even though his health and his physical constitution may have seemed frail. He radiated the confidence of a man who is tranquil and sure, like a child in the arms of his father. Meditating on the Gospel on Christmas night, he sketched his own portrait without knowing it: "The glory of God is peace. Wherever he is, there is peace.... He is with those of watchful hearts; with the humble and those who meet him at the level of his own 'height', the height of humility and love. To these people he gives his peace, so that through them, peace can enter this world."[4] We can understand this spiritual attitude as the secret of his courage. He knew that he was in his place. He experienced above him the benevolent and reassuring presence of the Eternal Father. One day, during a general audience, he confided how this reality touched and supported him every day:

> God is our Father, for him we are not anonymous, impersonal beings but have a name. And a phrase in the Psalms always moves me when I pray. "Your hands have made and fashioned me", says the Psalmist (Ps 119[118]:73). In this beautiful image each one of us can express his personal relationship with God. "Your hands have fashioned me. You thought of me and created and wanted me."[5]

[4] Homily at Midnight Mass, Christmas, Saint Peter's Square (December 24, 2008).
[5] General Audience (May 23, 2012).

In God's joy

To this quiet, confident faith we must add his childlike joy. I will never forget the smile of Benedict XVI! His luminous look spread gladness. He was a happy man. "Christianity is sometimes depicted as a way of life that stifles our freedom and goes against our desires for happiness and joy. But this is far from the truth. Christians are men and women who are truly happy because they know that they are not alone. They know that God is always holding them in his hands."[6]

How many times we saw his features drawn into a childlike smile! I remember the day in Castel Gandolfo, a place that he loved so much, when he had gone out onto the balcony to greet the crowd. He was so happy that he forgot a part of his address and a few moments later went back to make up for what he had omitted, smiling discreetly and good-naturedly about his distraction. Carried away again by his happiness, he forgot the blessing this time and went back again, gently and simply making fun of himself.

This joy was manifest during the liturgy. While contemplating the beauty of the rites that he had splendidly restored in Saint Peter's Basilica and listening to the magnificent sacred music that he had encouraged so much, the pope felt great satisfaction. Superficial observers will criticize a nostalgic attitude of an esthete. I think, rather, that we should see in it a mystical attitude, a contemplation of the divine intimacy through the liturgical beauty.

During these celebrations, Benedict XVI was perfectly recollected and manifestly happy, with a heavenly joy. He smiled gently to the concelebrants. I will never forget the

---

[6] Message of Pope Benedict XVI for the 27th World Youth Day (March 15, 2012).

day when he made a slight mistake in the intonation of a Gregorian chant *Gloria*, causing a few seconds of difficulty for the schola. Then he gave them a humble, simple smile, as though to ask their forgiveness. I understood then the secret of his joy: Benedict XVI did not take himself seriously. He took God seriously. In this, too, he was like a child in the presence of God. Children take their games seriously but do not take themselves seriously. Benedict XVI was one of them.

One day he explained why he was not a boring person but cheerful and pleasant. It was while meditating on the Immaculate Conception in 2005:

> [Sometimes] we have a lurking suspicion that a person who does not sin must really be basically boring and that something is missing from his life: the dramatic dimension of being autonomous; that the freedom to say no, to descend into the shadows of sin and to want to do things on one's own is part of being truly human; that only then can we make the most of all the vastness and depth of our being men and women, of being truly ourselves; that we should put this freedom to the test, even in opposition to God, in order to become, in reality, fully ourselves. In a word, we think that evil is basically good, we think that we need it, at least a little, in order to experience the fullness of being. We think that Mephistopheles—the tempter—is right when he says he is the power "that always wants evil and always does good" (Goethe, *Faust* I, 3). We think that a little bargaining with evil, keeping for oneself a little freedom against God, is basically a good thing, perhaps even necessary.
>
> If we look, however, at the world that surrounds us, we can see that this is not so [and] that evil is always poisonous, does not uplift human beings but degrades and humiliates them. It does not make them any the greater, purer, or wealthier, but harms and belittles them. This

is something we should indeed learn on the day of the Immaculate Conception: the person who abandons himself totally in God's hands does not become God's puppet, a boring "yes man"; he does not lose his freedom. Only the person who entrusts himself totally to God finds true freedom, the great, creative immensity of the freedom of good. The person who turns to God does not become smaller but greater, for through God and with God he becomes great, he becomes divine, he becomes truly himself. The person who puts himself in God's hands does not distance himself from others, withdrawing into his private salvation; on the contrary, it is only then that his heart truly awakens and he becomes a sensitive, hence, benevolent and open person. The closer a person is to God, the closer he is to people.[7]

Benedict XVI had this joyful freedom of a child who has said yes once for all and irrevocably to his Father and who becomes close to every human being.

Close to everyone

For this is the third feature that must be emphasized. Joseph Ratzinger, by his childlike spirit, knew how to become close to everyone. We should not reduce this fraternal, benevolent closeness to a psychological trait, a form of timidity, or else to the elegance of a German, perfectly civil education. No, his benevolence with everyone was the result of his entrance into the mystery of the divine childhood through the practice of the theological virtues.

[7] Homily on the Solemnity of the Immaculate Conception (December 8, 2005).

At Midnight Mass on Christmas 2008, he had emphasized:

> The medieval theologian William of Saint Thierry once said that God—from the time of Adam—saw that his grandeur provoked resistance in man, that we felt limited in our own being and threatened in our freedom. Therefore God chose a new way. He became a child. He made himself dependent and weak, in need of our love. Now—this God who has become a child says to us—you can no longer fear me, you can only love me.

What a revelation concerning the soul of Joseph Ratzinger! The sign of God, the thing that reveals his glory and omnipotence, is now the weakness of the infant! "God's sign is his humility. God's sign is that he makes himself small; he becomes a child; he lets us touch him, and he asks for our love. How we would prefer a different sign, an imposing, irresistible sign of God's power and greatness! But his sign summons us to faith and love ... this is what God is like. He has power, he is Goodness itself. He invites us to become like him."[8] Benedict XVI possessed intellectual, human, political power. But he was goodness itself. He was meek and humble. He became close to all like a child so as to be a sign of God in his weakness, so as to disarm fear and abolish distance. He embodied in his life this maxim of Master Eckhart: "The virtue named humility is rooted in the depths of the Deity."

Benedict XVI himself recounted how he discovered that someone who prays while saying "Our Father" is never alone: on the contrary, in experiencing the fatherhood of God, he enters into the great fraternity with all believers. And so, in commenting emotionally on the significance of

---

[8] Homily at Midnight Mass, Christmas, Saint Peter's Basilica (December 24, 2009).

the word Abba-Father with which we address God himself, he said:

> In praying our heart is opened; we enter into communion not only with God but actually with all the children of God, because we are one body. When we address the Father in our inner room in silence and in recollection, we are never alone. Those who speak to God are not alone. We are within the great prayer of the Church, we are part of a great symphony that the Christian community in all the parts of the earth and in all epochs raises to God. Naturally, the musicians and instruments differ—and this is an element of enrichment—but the melody of praise is one and in harmony. Every time, then, that we shout or say: "Abba! Father!" it is the Church, the whole communion of people in prayer, that supports our invocation, and our invocation is an invocation of the Church.[9]

Allow me to reminisce once again. I remember Pope Benedict during the entrance procession of a Midnight Mass. The Gregorian introit resounded: "Dominus dixit ad me, Filius meus es tu, ego hodie genuit te" (The Lord said to me: You are my Son, today I have begotten you). The vestments were magnificent. The heavy bronze baldachin by Bernini was decorated with flowers. Msgr. Guido Marini displayed all the splendor of the liturgy. The pope was tired but peaceful. His face radiated with a childlike joy. Covered with honors at the heart of the most beautiful edifice in all Christendom, he was the image of the Infant in the crib. He was the innocent, the disciple of the Prince of peace who was born that night. He had mystically entered into the relation of Son to the Father. To him the Father could say: "You are my son!" The concelebrating cardinals were

[9] General Audience (May 23, 2012).

seated. Something of the eternal liturgy was being anticipated before our eyes. It seemed that we could understand
how the eternal high priest was the innocent Lamb. After
the proclamation of the Gospel, the pope started the homily. His voice was worn but gentle. These unforgettable
words came straight from his heart:

> Again and again the beauty of this Gospel touches our
> hearts: a beauty that is the splendor of truth. Again and
> again it astonishes us that God makes himself a child so
> that we may love him, so that we may dare to love him,
> and as a child trustingly lets himself be taken into our arms.
> It is as if God were saying: I know that my glory frightens
> you and that you are trying to assert yourself in the face of
> my grandeur. So now I am coming to you as a child, so
> that you can accept me and love me.[10]

These words could have applied to him. The immensely
learned, powerful theologian made himself a child in God's
sight and in the sight of the whole Church so as to let himself be loved by the Father and by Christians.

What was the secret of his joy? He revealed it to us in
the continuation of this homily:

> God is glorious. God is pure light, the radiance of truth
> and love. He is good. He is true goodness, goodness *par
> excellence*. The angels surrounding him begin by simply
> proclaiming the joy of seeing God's glory. Their song
> radiates the joy that fills them. In their words, it is as if we
> were hearing the sounds of Heaven. There is no question
> of attempting to understand the meaning of it all, but sim-
> ply the overflowing happiness of seeing the pure splendor

[10] Homily at Midnight Mass, Christmas, Saint Peter's Basilica (December
24, 2012).

of God's truth and love. We want to let this joy reach out and touch us: truth exists, pure goodness exists, pure light exists. God is good, and he is the supreme power above all powers. All this should simply make us joyful tonight, together with the angels and the shepherds.

The pope's joy was not a passing gladness or a psychological euphoria. The cause of the joy of Benedict XVI was the contemplation of God himself. These words were like a foretaste by which he enjoyed the first fruits of Heaven. Benedict XVI allowed himself to be stirred by joy, the jubilation of the son that he was. He shared in the joy of the Eternal Son contemplating the goodness of the Almighty Father. He added these words in a voice trembling with emotion: "If God's light is extinguished, man's divine dignity is also extinguished. Then the human creature would cease to be God's image, to which we must pay honor in every person, in the weak, in the stranger, in the poor. Then we would no longer all be brothers and sisters, children of the one Father, who belong to one another on account of that one Father."

II

The Look of the Father

Contemplating the Eternal Father

As early as 1977, Joseph Ratzinger emphasized: being a father is possible "only if one accepts one's own status as a child". By entering spiritually into the intra-Trinitarian filial relation, Benedict himself became the father of all Christendom, the pope, the vicar of the Eternal Father on this earth. Few Supreme Pontiffs have taken this paternal sense as far as he did.

From his early years, Joseph Ratzinger contemplated the mystery of the Father, this question that has tormented the human heart since antiquity. He wrote:

> It is well known that the Greeks called their Zeus "Father". But this word was not an expression of their trust in him! Rather, it expressed the profound ambiguity of the god and the tragic ambiguity, indeed, the terrible character of the world. When they said "Father", they meant that Zeus was like human fathers—sometimes really nice, when he was in a good mood, but ultimately an egoist, a tyrant, unpredictable, unfathomable, and dangerous. And this was how they experienced the dark power that ruled the world: some individuals are courted as favorites, but this power stands by indifferently while other individuals starve to death, are enslaved, or go to

ruin. The "Father" of the world, as he is experienced in human life, reflects human fathers: partisan and, in the last analysis, terrible.[1]

This original and little-noted aspect of Joseph Ratzinger's thought must be emphasized. For him, observing human fathers is not the way to know what fatherhood is. The model of the Father is elsewhere. "The biblical Father is not a heavenly duplicate of human fatherhood. Rather, he posits something new: he is the divine critique of human fatherhood. God establishes his own criterion."[2] Benedict XVI would return to this many times, but especially in one of his last catecheses, on January 30, 2013, which resounds like a testament:

> At times communication [with a father] becomes difficult, trust is lacking, and the relationship with the father figure can become problematic; moreover, in this way even imagining God as a father becomes problematic.... Yet the revelation in the Bible helps us to overcome these difficulties by speaking to us of a God who shows us what it really means to be "father"; and it is the Gospel, especially, which reveals to us this face of God as a Father who loves, even to the point of giving his own Son....

We see that this idea structures Ratzinger's thought, and it does so as early as his book from 1977:

> God is—and the Christian faith adds: God is as Father, Son, and Holy Spirit, three and one. This is the very heart of Christianity, but it is so often shrouded in a silence born of perplexity. Has the Church perhaps gone one

[1] Joseph Ratzinger, *The God of Jesus Christ: Meditations on the Triune God*, trans. Brian McNeil (San Francisco: Ignatius Press, 2008), 32.
[2] Ibid., 33.

step too far here? Ought we not rather leave something so great and inaccessible as God in his inaccessibility? Can something like the Trinity have any real meaning for us? Well, it is certainly true that the proposition that "God is three and God is one" is and remains the expression of his otherness, which is infinitely greater than we and transcends all our thinking and our existence. But if this proposition had nothing to say to us, it would not have been revealed. And as a matter of fact, it could be clothed in human language only because it had already penetrated human thinking and living to some extent.

What, then, does this mean? Let us begin at the point where God himself began. He calls himself Father. Human fatherhood can give us an inkling of what God is; but where fatherhood no longer exists, where genuine fatherhood is no longer experienced as a phenomenon that goes beyond the biological dimension to embrace a human and intellectual sphere as well, it becomes meaningless to speak of God the Father. Where human fatherhood disappears, it is no longer possible to speak and think of God. It is not God who is dead; what is dead (at least to a large extent) is the precondition in man that makes it possible for God to live in the world. The crisis of fatherhood that we are experiencing today is a basic aspect of the crisis that threatens mankind as a whole.... If human existence is to be complete, we need a father, in the true meaning of fatherhood that our faith discloses.[3]

Before going any farther, it is necessary to underscore the current relevance of these words, which were written almost fifty years ago. What a prophetic vision! Note the shrewdness of the pastoral heart of Joseph Ratzinger. This is not a matter of metaphysical speculation. It took an exceptional capacity for discernment and tactful listening and a rare reliability of judgment to dare to formulate a diagnosis

[3] Ibid., 29–30.

that today seems irrefutable. It seems to me that we can see here the experience of the young religion teacher and the spiritual prudence of the assistant pastor hearing confessions in his parish during the first four years of his priestly ministry, from 1951 to 1955.

What, then, is this true fatherhood that the Bible reveals to us? Joseph Ratzinger defined it as follows: "a responsibility for one's child that does not dominate him but permits him to become his own self. This fatherhood is a love that [does not seek to take possession of the child. Nor does it abandon the child to his initial state under the pretext of respecting his freedom, but tries to lead the child to the innermost truth of his being, which he can find only in his Creator.]"[4] We could summarize it this way: fatherhood is defined as the responsibility to lead the other person, through love, to the truth of his being, without controlling him by violence.

In the image of the Almighty Father

This reflection would lead Benedict XVI to explore in greater depth the notion of God's fatherly omnipotence:

> His omnipotence is not expressed in violence, it is not expressed in the destruction of every adverse power as we might like; rather it is expressed in love, in mercy, in forgiveness, in accepting our freedom, and in the tireless call for conversion of heart, in an attitude only seemingly weak—God seems weak if we think of Jesus Christ who prays, who lets himself be killed. This apparently weak attitude consists of patience, meekness, and love, it shows that this is the real way to be powerful! This is God's power! And this power will win!... Only those who are truly

---

[4] Ibid., 30. The author revised and streamlined the citation.

powerful can tolerate evil and show compassion; only those who are truly powerful can fully exercise the force of love. And God, to whom all things belong because all things were made by him, shows his power by loving everything and everyone, patiently waiting for the conversion of us human beings, whom he wants to be his children.... The omnipotence of love is not that of worldly power but is that of the total gift, and Jesus, the Son of God, reveals to the world the true omnipotence of the Father.[5]

These words are extremely important theologically; they correct and put in order the erroneous arguments in theologies about the weakness of God, the divine withdrawal, or the end of omnipotence. They also bring to light the right intentions that motivated them. They allow us to enter into the contemplation of the Eternal Father by Benedict XVI.

Here we can understand profoundly what some have called the "political weakness" of his pontificate. Benedict XVI did not act as a politician. He did not appoint more and more cardinals so as to tilt the balance in a future conclave, although he knew the date of the next one. He did not exclude his adversaries. On the contrary, he was patient to the end. This attitude has been attributed to a psychological inability to act severely, to make decisions, to punish. Until the end of his earthly life, he bore with weakness and incompetency, even in his coworkers. Was this out of timidity? On the contrary, I think that it was instead out of a mystical desire to enter into the fatherly exercise of power as God teaches it to us.

This choice allowed for no compromise. He knew that he was Father and therefore responsible for bringing everyone to the full truth of his being. He felt responsible for the truth. This is why he never gave in to the wolves.

[5] Benedict XVI, General Audience (January 30, 2013).

His fatherhood gave him heroic courage to confront the packs unleashed by the media and the mockery coming from the Catholic world.

In 2009 he welcomed with a fatherly heart the faithful who had come from Anglicanism wanting to return to Catholic unity. He permitted them to preserve the best of their liturgical tradition, recalling then that

> every division among the baptized in Jesus Christ wounds that which the Church is and that for which the Church exists; in fact, "such division openly contradicts the will of Christ, scandalizes the world, and damages the holy cause of preaching the Gospel to every creature."[6] Precisely for this reason, before shedding his blood for the salvation of the world, the Lord Jesus prayed to the Father for the unity of his disciples.[7]

The unity of all in the Church is a gift from the heart of the Eternal Father. Benedict XVI experienced all division as a wound inflicted on his own fatherly heart.

Therefore he suffered immensely when, that same year, he was dragged through the mud by some Catholics for having dared to offer gestures of unity with dissident Christian communities. He wrote a personal letter to the bishops in which his fatherly heart spoke with a heartrending sincerity:

> Leading men and women to God, to the God who speaks in the Bible: this is the supreme and fundamental priority of the Church and of the Successor of Peter at the present time. A logical consequence of this is that we must have at heart the unity of all believers.... That the quiet gesture

---

[6] Vatican Council II, Decree on Ecumenism *Unitatis redintegratio* (November 21, 1964), no. 1.

[7] Apostolic Constitution *Anglicanorum coetibus* (November 4, 2009).

of extending a hand gave rise to a huge uproar ... is a fact
which we must accept. But I ask now: Was it, and is it,
truly wrong in this case to meet half-way the brother ...
and to seek reconciliation?

The pope goes on to mention the separated communities
that include so many priests and seminarians.

We cannot know how mixed their motives may be. All
the same, I do not think that they would have chosen the
priesthood if, alongside various distorted and unhealthy
elements, they did not have a love for Christ and a desire
to proclaim him and, with him, the living God. Can we
simply exclude them, as representatives of a radical fringe,
from our pursuit of reconciliation and unity? What would
then become of them?[8]

The whole letter reveals the heart of a father concerned
about each of his children, responsible for their ascent
toward the full truth of their being. No compromise with
error, no complicit silence, but rather acceptance of his
responsibility of fatherly mercy. All divisive activity, all
rejection, and all exclusion of a brother whom one labels a
traditionalist is a work of the devil.

Nowadays when, under the pretext of being an inclu-
sive and synodal Church, people go so far as to silence
the truth at the same time and to exclude persons in the
name of consensus, we ought to meditate on this example. Think about the recent bullying of Catholics who
are attached to the Extraordinary Form of the Roman
Rite. While Pope Francis, as a good father, encourages

---

[8] Letter to the Bishops of the Catholic Church concerning the Remission
of the Excommunication of the Four Bishops Consecrated by Archbishop
Lefebvre (March 10, 2009).

the bishops to take a benevolent attitude, some members of the Curia, who ought to love the liturgy, contradict him and are trying to prevent the bishops from acting according to their fatherly heart. Wolves prowl around the pope and by their decisions distort his fatherly face. In conscience and in the sight of God, the bishops must take their responsibility as fathers: the responsibility to lead everyone to the most intimate truth of his being. In the Name of God, from whom all fatherhood comes, may the bishops be fathers and not tyrants or simple managers! More than ever the words of Benedict XVI ought to challenge us: "Perhaps people today fail to perceive the beauty, greatness, and profound consolation contained in the word 'father' with which we can turn to God in prayer because today the father figure is often not sufficiently present and all too often is not sufficiently positive in daily life."[9] What is true in the life of families is true also in the life of the Church. Whatever the liturgy may be in which they practice their faith, Christians need priests who are for them the image of the Heavenly Father. Priests aspire to find in their bishop a true father for their soul. The Church suffers from the absence of truly fatherly hearts that could make us enter into the experience of God's fatherly gaze at us.

Entering into the divine fatherhood

This benevolent, fatherly gaze is a participation in "God's fatherhood [which] is infinite love, tenderness that bends over us, frail children, in need of everything".[10] I think I

[9] General Audience (May 23, 2012).
[10] General Audience (January 30, 2013).

can say that here we are in the presence of a major feature of the soul of Benedict XVI. I can even state that his mystic life rises to the surface behind these words. Everyone knows the man's discretion, gentleness, and humility. He never wanted to display this secret of his heart for everyone to see.

However, one day the door opened partly, and he let us see the innermost recesses of his spiritual life. It was during a homily on the occasion of his eightieth birthday, on April 15, 2007. We were struck by an unexpected confidence: "Yes, I thank God because ... I have been able to experience what 'fatherhood' means, so that the words about God as Father were made understandable to me from within; on the basis of human experience, access was opened to me to the great and benevolent Father who is in Heaven." Truly, Benedict XVI had a mystical experience of the divine fatherhood. His whole personality was shaped by this mystery. He became a temporal reflection of the Eternal Father.

The bread of truth

This strong, gentle fatherhood was expressed clearly in his homily during the Mass for the inauguration of his pontificate:

> One of the basic characteristics of a shepherd must be to love the people entrusted to him, even as he loves Christ whom he serves. "Feed my sheep," says Christ to Peter, and now, at this moment, he says it to me as well. Feeding means loving, and loving also means being ready to suffer. Loving means giving the sheep what is truly good, the nourishment of God's truth, of God's word, the nourishment of his presence, which he gives us in the Blessed Sacrament.

Here Pope Benedict reveals to us the root of his courage. He is ready to suffer in order to feed his children. He wants to lead them to the truth, to feed them with the truth. For the truth is the bread of the father. It is this food that the father gives to each one. The expression used here is striking: "the nourishment of God's truth". It helps us to understand the extent to which, for Joseph Ratzinger, the truth is not an ideology or a concept. It is this vitally necessary bread. In giving the truth to the faithful, he imposes nothing on them by force; he offers them the means of carrying out their freedom. Concern for the truth is, in the teaching of Benedict XVI, the mark of his fatherly love.

> Our faith is decisively opposed to the attitude of resignation that considers man incapable of truth—as if this were more than he could cope with. This attitude of resignation with regard to truth, I am convinced, lies at the heart of the crisis of the West, the crisis of Europe. If truth does not exist for man, then neither can he ultimately distinguish between good and evil. And then the great and wonderful discoveries of science become double-edged: they can open up significant possibilities for good, for the benefit of mankind, but also, as we see only too clearly, they can pose a terrible threat, involving the destruction of man and the world. We need truth. Yet admittedly, in the light of our history we are fearful that faith in the truth might entail intolerance.... [Nevertheless,] truth prevails not through external force, but it is humble and it yields itself to man only via the inner force of its veracity. Truth proves itself in love. It is never our property, never our product, just as love can never be produced, but only received and handed on as a gift. We need this inner force of truth. As Christians we trust this force of truth. We are its witnesses. We must hand it on as a gift in the same way as we have received it, as it has given itself to us.[11]

[11] Homily in Mariazell (September 8, 2007).

And so Joseph Ratzinger's love for truth should not be attributed to a professorial intellectual obsession or to a psychological difficulty, much less to authoritarian rigidity. All those who knew him know how simple and intellectually benevolent he was. For my part, I think that this love for the truth originated in his gradual entrance into the mystery of the Eternal Father. Just as the Father begets the uncreated Word, the ultimate and perfect Truth, so too every father, and to the highest degree the Holy Father, is duty-bound to offer to all the divine truth and the inviolable doctrinal and moral teaching of the Church. Woe to the fathers who would deprive their children of truth in the name of an artificial tolerance. Those fathers are in danger of reaping one day the anger of their children whom they abandoned to a counterfeit of freedom. Let us be grateful to Benedict XVI, who offered to everyone abundantly "the nourishment of the divine truth"! Through his teaching, he begat children, educated young souls, strengthened minds.

His posterity will be like that of Abraham, the father of believers: numerous and beautiful. The seed that he sowed will spring up in abundance. From the height of Heaven, he will see the harvest.

Father of contemplatives

After his death, several people close to Benedict XVI reported that one of the great joys of his life had been to know that his pontificate had led to a great movement of contemplative vocations. Benedict XVI loved monks as the hidden treasures of the Church: "Every monastery ... is an oasis in which the deep well, from which to draw 'living water' to quench our deepest thirst, is constantly being dug with prayer and meditation", he said at the Charterhouse of Serra San Bruno on October 9, 2011.

In this sense, we can say that Joseph Ratzinger saw monasteries as the typical realization of the Church. They are, in miniature, what the Church is on a large scale. Indeed, the chief characteristic of a monastery is summed up in a sentence from the Rule of Saint Benedict that Joseph Ratzinger quoted so many times: "Place nothing at all before the Work of God", in other words, nothing should have priority over God; we must put him concretely in first place. Now, for Benedict XVI, this point is the fundamental rule of every Christian life. "God is the highest priority. If anything in our life deserves haste without delay, then it is God's work alone.... God is ... the most important thing in our lives."[12]

Benedict XVI was a father for consecrated religious, for monks in particular, because he constantly reminded them of the heart of their identity by holding it up as an example to the whole Church, as, for instance, during the visit that he made to the Cistercians in Heiligenkreuz on September 9, 2007:

> In the life of monks, however, prayer takes on a particular importance: it is the heart of their calling. Their vocation is to be men of prayer. In the patristic period the monastic life was likened to the life of the angels. It was considered the essential mark of the angels that they are worshippers. Their very life is worship. This should hold true also for monks. Monks pray first and foremost, not for any specific intention, but simply because God is worthy of being praised. "Confitemini Domino, quoniam bonus!" (Praise the Lord, for he is good, for his mercy

[12] Homily at Midnight Mass, Christmas, Saint Peter's Square (December 24, 2009).

is eternal!): so we are urged by a number of Psalms (e.g., Ps 106:1). Such prayer for its own sake, intended as pure divine service, is rightly called *officium*. It is "service" par excellence, the "sacred service" of monks. It is offered to the triune God who, above all else, is worthy "to receive glory, honor and power" (Rev 4:11), because he wondrously created the world and even more wondrously renewed it.... Dear friends, make this priority given to God very apparent to people! As a spiritual oasis, a monastery reminds today's world of the most important and, indeed, in the end, the only decisive thing: that there is an ultimate reason why life is worth living: God and his unfathomable love.

The father of priests

In the book *For Eternity*, I described the extraordinary paternal kindness with which Benedict XVI loved priests. The reader will find several testimonies to it in this book. Twice I saw his fatherly love for priests lead him to shed tears.

The first time was on June 10, 2010, when, in the middle of more than ten thousand priests gathered on Saint Peter's Square, he was moved to tears by their filial love. I will never forget the infinite gentleness of his words. He mentioned the joy that he shared in common with them of being a priest and thanked them while asking them for one thing only: "Be passionate for Christ.... Be full of the joy of the Gospel!" How gently he made the point, yet how forcefully he hammered it home: "Do not neglect your own soul.... Prayer is not a marginal thing [i.e., not optional but the heart of the priest's life]: it is the priest's job to pray, as representative of the people who do not know how to pray or do not find time to pray." How kindly he smiled as he told them: "Have the humility,

the courage to rest. [That is part of your priestly work.]"
Next he mentioned his memories of his years of study and
recalled humorously that the heterodox hypotheses of his
youth had long since fallen into oblivion. Then he added:
"We must have the courage ... and ... the humility not to
submit to all the hypotheses of the moment and to live by
the great faith of the Church of all times.... Trust in the
... Church ... and in the *Catechism of the Catholic Church*"
as an absolutely sure theological criterion.

As the evening went on, Benedict XVI opened his
fatherly heart more and more. At one point he became
more animated, his eyes gleamed as though he could see
what he was talking about: "We must allow ourselves
to be drawn so as to enter into the 'I' of Christ. This
is what celibacy is, letting oneself be penetrated by the
'I' of Christ. The major problem with today's world is
that people no longer think about the eternal world that
is to come. The celibacy of the priest cracks open a door
to the future world." He went on, his voice becoming stronger: "Celibacy will always be a scandal for the
world. The world critiques the celibacy because it wants
to do away with the reality of the Lord!" Ten thousand
priests started to applaud vigorously. A father had put
into words so accurately the profound aspiration of their
soul: "Celibacy is a definitive yes. It is to let oneself be
taken in the hand of God.... It is the definitive yes, a yes
to the future world. It is a scandal to the world, because it
is a life staked entirely on God. It is a great sign of God's
presence in the world." The priests were happy, many
wept for spiritual joy. They felt that they were understood, loved, and comforted. Benedict XVI proposed to
them that evening the true remedy to clericalism: "Living the Eucharist in its true depth will make us go out of
ourselves so as to enter into the communion of the one

Father. The Eucharist is the opposite of being closed in on oneself."

How could I fail to recall the words that he addressed to the Austrian priests?

> Your primary service to this world must therefore be your prayer and the celebration of the Divine Office. The interior disposition of each priest, and of each conse-crated person, must be that of "putting nothing before the Divine Office". The beauty of this inner attitude will find expression in the beauty of the liturgy, so that wherever we join in singing, praising, exalting, and worshipping God, a little bit of Heaven will become present on earth. Truly it would not be presumptuous to say that, in a lit-urgy completely centered on God, we can see, in its rituals and chant, an image of eternity.... In all our efforts on behalf of the liturgy, the determining factor must always be our looking to God. We stand before God—he speaks to us and we speak to him. Whenever in our thinking we are only concerned about making the liturgy attractive, interesting, and beautiful, the battle is already lost. Either it is *Opus Dei*, with God as its specific subject, or it is not. In the light of this, I ask you to celebrate the sacred liturgy with your gaze fixed on God within the communion of saints, the living Church of every time and place, so that it will truly be an expression of the sublime beauty of the God who has called men and women to be his friends.[13]

On that same evening in 2010, on Saint Peter's Square, he asked himself what we ought to do about the vocations crisis. "The temptation to take things into our own hands is great, the temptation to transform the priesthood into ... a 'job' with specific working hours.... But this is a temp-tation that does not solve the problem." The priesthood

---

[13] Address at Heiligenkreuz Abbey (September 9, 2007).

has a sacred character that comes from God because it is a vocation! He then mentioned the figures of priests who had led him to aspire to the priesthood, and he exhorted his listeners to challenge young men: "Do you think that you might become a priest?"

The father of children

Benedict XVI was always sensitive to the question of catechizing.

The *Catechism of the Catholic Church* is his great work. Remember also his conferences on this subject throughout the world. Is this a professorial hobby horse? A personal interest? On the contrary, what is revealed here is a fatherly heart, a childlike soul. As proof of this, we cite the conference that he gave on December 10, 2000,[14] to catechists from all over the world in which he recalled that evangelization involves the whole life of the priest, and not only his words. Here Joseph Ratzinger revealed the innermost driving force of his life. We can read it as a prophecy of his pontificate and of its future fruitfulness:

> "I have come in my Father's name, and you do not receive me; if another comes in his own name, him you will receive", the Savior said (Jn 5:43). The distinctive sign of the Antichrist is that he speaks in his own name. The sign of the Son is his communion with the Father. The Son introduces us into the Trinitarian communion, into the circle of eternal love, of which the Persons are "pure relations", the pure act of giving oneself and receiving each other. The Trinitarian plan—visible in the Son, who does

[14]Joseph Ratzinger, "The New Evangelization" (address, Convention of Catechists and Religion Teachers, Vatican City, December 10, 2000).

not speak in his own name—shows the way of life of a
true evangelizer—better yet, evangelizing is not just a way
of speaking, but a way of living: a life of listening and of
becoming the Father's voice: "He will not speak on his
own authority, but whatever he hears he will speak", the
Lord says concerning the Holy Spirit (Jn 16:13).

Some very practical consequences follow from this law.
All reasonable and morally acceptable methods must be
studied—it is a duty to utilize these possibilities of communication. But words and all the art of communication
cannot reach the human person at the depth where the
Gospel should arrive. Several years ago, I was reading the
biography of an excellent priest of our [twentieth] century, Dom Didimo, a parish priest in Bassano del Grappa.
Among his notes we find invaluable words, the fruit of a
life of prayer and meditation. On this subject, for example,
Dom Didimo says: "Jesus preached by day, and by night
he prayed." With this brief remark he meant: Jesus had to
acquire his disciples from God. This is always valid. We
ourselves cannot win human beings over. We must obtain
them from God for God. All methods are empty without
the foundation of prayer. The word of proclamation must
always be immersed in an intense prayer life.

To this we must add an additional element. Jesus
preached by day, by night he prayed—but that is not all.
His entire life—as the Gospel of Saint Luke shows very
beautifully—was a journey to the Cross, an ascent to
Jerusalem. Jesus did not redeem the world by fine words,
but by his suffering and death. His Passion is a source of
inexhaustible life for the world; his Passion gives power
to his words....

Saint Augustine says the same thing in a more beautiful way while interpreting John 21, where the prophecy
of Peter's martyrdom is closely connected with the com-
mand to feed the sheep, in other words, the institution of
his primacy. Saint Augustine comments as follows on the
verse John 21:16: "Feed my sheep", in other words, suffer

for my sheep (*Sermo Guelf.* 32 PLS 2, 640). A mother cannot give life to a child without suffering. Every childbirth involves suffering, is suffering, and becoming Christian is a childbirth. We can put it in the Lord's words: the Kingdom of Heaven suffers violence (Mt 11:12; Lk 16:16), but God's violence is suffering, it is the Cross. We cannot give life to others without giving our life. Recall the Savior's words: "Whoever loses his life for my sake and the gospel's will save it" (Mk 8:35).

To conclude, I would like to mention October 15, 2005, the day when Benedict XVI met thousands of children from the parishes of Latium who were about to make their First Holy Communion. I think that I had never seen the pope so glad, literally radiant with joy and happiness. He was surrounded by the children, who were seated all around his chair. They asked their questions in naïve, touching words. The Holy Father became a catechist, like a rural parish priest. The first question was: "What are your memories of your First Communion day?" Benedict XVI emotionally told about the moment when "Jesus entered my heart ... and took me by the hand.... It was the beginning of a journey together, a lifelong friendship with Jesus." The next questions were: "Jesus is present in the Eucharist. But how? I can't see him!" The pope took the question seriously, very affectionately, and explained pedagogically that many things exist but are not seen. The Holy Father found simple, precise words, and the children listened to him, fascinated. What a marvel: this immensely talented theologian, this instructor who correctly and rigorously answered the questions from the children in a few sentences. Evening fell on that place; time was suspended. One had the impression of seeing Jesus again surrounded by children. He was at the same time the child in the midst of the

children and the Father surrounded by the little ones that
God had given to him as sons and daughters.

This spiritual participation in the divine fatherhood
was also practiced by Benedict XVI in a very hidden way
through his love for the sick and the poor. His extreme
modesty led him to live out this paternal love discreetly.
His visits to sick children were not broadcast by the media.
They were, however, an opportunity to discover the tenderness of which he was capable. Once again, this aspect of
his personality was not the result of a human predisposition.
On the contrary, his own shyness and reserve might have
put him at a loss. We should interpret it instead as looking
at suffering through the eyes of faith, a look that merges
with that of the Heavenly Father upon the poor and the
little ones. We remember in particular a visit to the pedi-
atric ward at the Gemelli Polyclinic on January 8, 2011.
The pope went into each room; he offered a gift and a
smile. The children were happy and proud. Benedict XVI
then found himself face to face with a little boy who was
crying bitterly. For a moment he was paralyzed by emotion. He approached and delicately put a marionette into
the boy's hands. Their eyes met. The father's look rested
on the child, who stopped crying and smiled. The pope
embraced him with the kindness of a father. A little farther on, two nurses presented to the Holy Father an infant
girl who had been born a year earlier with a very serious
cerebral malformation. She was so disfigured that her parents had abandoned her at birth. The nurses on the ward
had adopted her and took turns caring for her lovingly.
The pope, very moved, went over to her. He caressed the
infant's cheek with infinite respect. "You are beautiful,"
he murmured, "you will be blessed forever." There is an
obvious connection with the stories that Joseph Ratzinger
confided one day concerning the horror he had felt as a

youth when the mentally handicapped were eliminated by the Nazi regime.

> The small piece of property which was next to our house had previously been cultivated by three unmarried brothers to whom it belonged. It was alleged that they were mentally ill even though in actual fact they were able to look after their house and their property. They also disappeared into an institution, and soon afterward it was made known that they had died. At this point there could no longer be any doubt about what was happening—a systematic elimination of all those who were not considered productive was being carried out. The State had arrogated to itself the right to decide who deserved to live and who was to be deprived of the right to exist on the grounds of advantage to the community or to the state, employing as a criterion the idea that an individual could be eliminated because he was not useful to others or to himself. This fact added a new and different kind of anxiety to the horrors of war, which were themselves becoming ever more deeply felt—we were touched by the chilling coldness of a logic based upon criteria of utility and power. We felt that the killing of these people humiliated and threatened us, the human essence that was within us: if patience and love dedicated to the suffering are eliminated from human existence because they are seen as a waste of time and money, not only do we do wrong to those who are killed, but those who survive are themselves mutilated in their spirits. We realized that when the mystery of God—his inviolable dignity, which is present in each and every man—is not respected, then not only are individuals threatened, but humanity itself is endangered.[15]

[15]Joseph Cardinal Ratzinger, "The Likeness of God in the Human Being" (opening address, Eleventh International Conference Organized by the Pontifical Council for Pastoral Assistance and Health Care Workers, Vatican City, November 28–30, 1996).

Beyond the horrors that these memories inspired in the Bavarian pope, it seems to me that Joseph Ratzinger developed an ability to contemplate Christ crucified in every suffering person. I think that I can say that he wanted to look at every patient in the way in which God the Father looked at Christ on the Cross. This look, an altogether providential endowment, infinitely surpasses mere human emotion. It is a look of fatherly and divine compassion. He himself explained it clearly:

The Crucified thus becomes the living "icon of love". Precisely in the Crucified, in his flayed and beaten face, man once again becomes the transparency of God, the image of God that shines forth anew. In this way the light of divine love lies specifically upon suffering people, in whom the splendor of the creation has been externally dimmed. Because these people are in a special way similar to the crucified Christ, to the icon of love, they have drawn near to a special shared nature with him who, alone, is the image of God. We can say of them, as Tertullian said of Christ, "However wretched his body may be ..., it will always be my Christ" (*Adversus Marcionem* III, 17, 2). However great their suffering may be, however disfigured or dimmed their human existence may be, they will always be the favorite children of our Lord and they will always be his image in a special way. Taking the tension between the hidden and future manifestation of the image of God as our point of departure, we can apply the words of the First Letter of John to the question we have posed: "We are children of God even now, and what we shall be hereafter has not been made known as yet" (3:2). In all human beings—but especially in those who suffer—we love what they shall be and what in reality they already are. They are already children of God—they are in the image of Christ even though what they will become is not yet manifest. Christ on the Cross likened himself in definitive fashion to the poorest, the most defenseless, the most abandoned, and the most despised. And among these there are ... those whose rational soul is unable to express itself perfectly because of an infirm or sick brain, as though, for one reason or another, matter were resisting being taken up by the spirit. Here Jesus reveals the essence of humanity, that which is its real fulfillment—not intelligence or beauty, and even less wealth or pleasure, but the ability to love and to consent lovingly to the will of the Father, however disconcerting this may be.…

But I would like here to bear witness to the love the Church bears toward those who suffer mentally. Yes, the Church loves you. She not only bears toward you that natural "preference" borne by mothers toward the most suffering of their children. She adopts a stance of admiration not only toward what you will be, but also toward what you are now: images of Christ. Images of Christ who should be honored, respected, helped to the utmost, certainly, but, above all, images of Christ who are bearers of an essential message about the truth of man. A message that we tend to forget too often: our value in the eyes of God does not depend upon intelligence, stability of character, or the health that enables us to engage in many actions of generosity. These elements could disappear at any moment. Our value in the eyes of God depends solely upon the choice we have taken to love as much as possible, to love as much as possible in truth. To say that God has created us in his image means that he wanted each one of us to express an aspect of his infinite splendor, that he has a design for each of us, that each of us is destined to enter—by means of an itinerary that is specific to him—into blessed eternity.[16]

Benedict XVI was like that. He had a fatherly look and a childlike smile. He was a reflection of the Father on this earth, an image of the innocent Son. He will remain the father of our souls for a long time.

[16] Ibid.

Part Two

Faces of the Pontificate

I

Benedict XVI, My Friend

Article published on January 4, 2023,
in *Le Figaro* on the occasion of the
death of Joseph Ratzinger

For most commentators, Benedict XVI will be remembered as an immensely gifted intellectual. His work will endure. His homilies have already become classics, like those of the Fathers of the Church. But to those who have had the grace to collaborate closely with him, Pope Benedict XVI left much more than writings and documents. I think that I can say that every meeting with him was a genuine spiritual experience that left its mark on my soul. Together they compose a spiritual portrait of someone whom I regard as a saint, and I hope that he will soon be canonized and declared a Doctor of the Church.

When I arrived at the Roman Curia in 2001 as a young archbishop—I was then fifty-five years old—I observed and admired the perfect understanding between John Paul II and the man who was then Cardinal Ratzinger. They were so completely united that it was impossible for them to be separated one from the other. John Paul II was filled with wonder at the depth of Joseph Ratzinger. For his part, the cardinal was fascinated by the extent to which John Paul II was immersed in God. Both of them sought God and wished to restore to the world a taste for this quest.

Joseph Ratzinger was recognized as a man of great sensitivity and modesty. I never saw him display the slightest contempt. On the contrary, even when he was immersed in work, he made himself completely available to listen to his interlocutor. If he got the impression that he had offended someone, he always tried to explain to him the reasons for his position. He was incapable of a cutting remark or gesture. I must say also that he showed great respect for the African theologians. He even gladly agreed to render them practical services or to pass a message on to John Paul II. This profound benevolence and respectful tact toward everyone are characteristics of Joseph Ratzinger.

From 2008 on, I replaced Cardinal Dias, Prefect of the Congregation for the Evangelization of Peoples, at a number of meetings because he was suffering from a debilitating illness. In this context, I had the chance to participate in many work sessions with Pope Benedict XVI. In particular, I had to present to him the draft nominations of bishops from more than a thousand dioceses in mission lands. We sometimes had rather long sessions, lasting much more than an hour. It was necessary to discuss and weigh delicate situations. Some countries lived under a system of persecution. Other dioceses were in crisis. I was struck by the humility of Benedict XVI and his ability to listen. I think that he always trusted his coworkers. That, incidentally, earned him some betrayals and disappointments. But Benedict XVI was so incapable of dissimulation that he could not believe that a man of the Church would be capable of lying. Choosing personnel was not easy for him.

From these long, repeated conversations, I gained a better understanding of the soul of the Bavarian pope. He had a perfect trust in God, which gave him a tranquil peace and continuous joy. John Paul II sometimes displayed holy anger. Benedict XVI always remained calm. He was sometimes wounded and suffered profoundly to see souls stray from God. He was lucid about the state of the Church. Yet a peaceful strength dwelt within him. He knew that the truth cannot be negotiated. In this sense, he did not like the political aspect of his office. I was always struck by the luminous joy in his eyes. Moreover, he had a sense of humor that was very gentle, never violent or vulgar.

I remember the Year of the Priest that he had decreed in 2010. The pope wished to emphasize the theological and mystical roots of the priestly life. He had truthfully and courageously confronted the first revelations concerning incidents of pedophilia in the clergy. He wanted to get to the bottom of the problem so as to purify the Church. That year culminated in a magnificent vigil on Saint Peter's Square. The setting sun flooded the Bernini colonnade with a golden light. The esplanade was packed. Unlike the usual crowds, though, there were no families, no nuns; just men, just priests. When Benedict XVI arrived in the popemobile, with one accord they all started to cheer him and call him by name. It was thrilling, all those manly voices chanting in unison: "Benedetto". The pope was very moved. When he turned toward the crowd after going up onto the platform, tears were streaming down his face. They brought him the prepared speech, which he set aside, and instead he answered questions impromptu. What a marvelous moment! The father, full of wisdom, taught his children. It seemed that time stood still. Benedict XVI confided in them. That evening he spoke definitive words about priestly celibacy. Then the evening ended with a long moment of adoration of the Blessed Sacrament, because Benedict XVI always wanted to lead those whom he met to prayer.

Benedict XVI loved priests passionately. The crisis of the priesthood and the purification of the priesthood were his daily Way of the Cross. He loved to meet priests and to speak familiarly with them.

He particularly loved seminarians, also. He was rarely happier than when surrounded by all those theology students who reminded him of his years as a young professor. I remember that memorable meeting with seminarians from the United States, during which Benedict XVI joked with them and burst out laughing. When they chanted, "We love you", the pope's voice broke, and he told them with fatherly emotion: "I pray for you every day."

Prayer and adoration were central to his pontificate. Who can forget the World Youth Day in Madrid? The pope was radiant with joy in front of an enthusiastic crowd of more than a million young people from all over the world. The communion among them all was tangible. At the moment when he started his speech, a terrible storm broke out. The backdrop was in danger of collapsing, and the wind had carried off the Holy Father's white skullcap. His entourage wanted to bring him to shelter. He refused. He smiled under a driving rain, from which a poor umbrella scarcely protected him. He smiled while looking at that crowd in the wind and the storm. He remained to the end. When the elements calmed down, the master of ceremonies brought him the text that he was supposed to read, but he preferred to omit the prepared speech so as not to encroach on the time scheduled for Eucharistic adoration. A few moments after the storm, the pope was kneeling before the Blessed Sacrament, leading the crowd in an impressive, fervent silence.

In 2010, Benedict XVI had instructed the secretary of state, Tarcisio Cardinal Bertone, to inform me that I would be created a cardinal at the Consistory in November 2010.

Incidentally, he is the same secretary of state who had announced to me on October 7, 2010, that Benedict XVI was appointing me president of the Pontifical Council *Cor unum* (the dicastery in charge of works of charity). Upon my return from India, therefore, I had the joy and the privilege of meeting Benedict XVI in a private audience. I was anxious to thank him for the cardinalate, but above all for having entrusted to me the Pontifical Council *Cor unum* and the heavy responsibility of putting into action his encyclical *Deus caritas est*, which states that "the Church's deepest nature is expressed in her threefold responsibility of: proclaiming the word of God (*kerygma-martyria*), celebrating the sacraments (*leitourgia*), and exercising the ministry of charity (*diakonia*). These duties presuppose each other and are inseparable." I will never forget the reason that he gave to me for it: "I appointed you because I know that you have experience of suffering and of the face of poverty. You will be the best capable to express tactfully the compassion and the closeness of the Church with the poorest of the poor." Benedict XVI had a profound Christian sense of suffering. He often repeated that humanity's greatness lies in its capacity to suffer for love of the truth. In this sense, Benedict XVI is great! He never retreated when faced with suffering. He never retreated when confronted by the wolves. Some sought to silence him. He was never afraid. His resignation in 2013 was the product not of discouragement but rather of the certitude that he would serve the Church more effectively by silence and prayer.

After my appointment by Pope Francis as prefect for divine worship in November 2014, I still had the occasion to meet the pope emeritus several times. I knew how close the question of the liturgy was to his heart. Therefore I often consulted him. He vigorously encouraged me several times—indeed, he was convinced that "the renewal of the liturgy is a fundamental prerequisite for the renewal of the Church."

I brought him my books. He read them and gave his evaluation. Moreover, he was willing to write the preface for [the French edition of] *The Power of Silence*. I remember the day when I announced to him my intention to write a book about the crisis of the Church. On that day he was tired, but his look brightened. You had to know the look of Benedict XVI in order to understand. It was the joyous, luminous look of a child, full of kindness and meekness and yet filled with strength and encouragement. I would never have written without that encouragement. A little later, we would collaborate closely with a view to publishing our reflection on priestly celibacy. I will keep in the secrecy of my heart the details of those unforgettable days. I will keep in the depths of my memory his great suffering and his tears, but also his fierce, unshaken determination not to give in to lies.

What kind of a portrait do these memories sketch? I think that they converge on the image of the Good Shepherd, which Benedict XVI loved so much. He did not want any of his sheep to be lost. He wanted to feed them with the truth and not to abandon them to the wolves or to errors. But above all, he loved them. Benedict XVI loved souls. He loved them because they had been entrusted to him by Christ. And most of all, he passionately loved this Jesus to whom he decided to dedicate the three volumes of his masterpiece, *Jesus of Nazareth*. Benedict XVI loved the one who is the life, the way, and the Truth.

II

The Future of the Church
Depends on the Liturgy

Article published in *Il Timone*, February 2023

The pontificate of Benedict XVI will go down in history, because of the contribution of this cultivated, refined theologian—certainly the most important one of the twentieth century—to a more serious and, I would say, definitive reflection on the liturgy and its consequences in the life of the Church.

As a protagonist and the supreme interpreter of Vatican Council II and its documents, Benedict XVI developed the profound conviction that "the liturgy is the source and summit of the life of the Church" (cf. *Sacrosanctum concilium*, 10). Throughout his continual theological reflection, this conviction grew more and more. In his mature works, he could write that the future of the Church depends on the liturgy: "The Church stands and falls with the liturgy."[1] Indeed, the credible presence of the Church in the world depends on the way in which she lives out this vital relation with her *lex orandi* [law of prayer].

The powerful theological reflection of Benedict XVI on the *lex credendi* [law of faith] was mixed with a no less

[1] Preface to *Die heilige Liturgie*, ed. Franz Breid (Steyr, Austria: Ennsthaler Verlag, 1997).

significant reflection on the Church's *lex orandi*. As Pastor of the Universal Church, he made his pontificate a continuous liturgy, both in the liturgical celebrations and in the various moments when, through words and gestures, he was called to testify to the Church's faith and to proclaim it.

His Magisterium was imbued with the liturgy, celebrated and explained in the manner of the ancient Fathers of the Church, who turned each one of their celebrations into a living mystagogy so as to initiate countless generations of Christians to the faith and to form them in it.

Benedict XVI understood that one cannot separate the faith that is received in the act of believing from the faith that is actualized in the works of one's life. The faith that is believed, the faith that prays, and the faith that is lived out are inseparable. He tried to make us understand that the more the faith makes itself prayer, the firmer it is. The more it becomes a praying faith, along the lines of the perennial tradition of the Church, the more correctly and strongly one adheres to it.

When he became pontiff and Universal Pastor of the Church, Benedict XVI reminded the Church about the beauty, the centrality, and the sacred character of the liturgy in Christian life, particularly in the life of priests. A centrality that is a Presence, that speaks about an Other, about the true Protagonist of the liturgical action, that speaks about the true center of the Church and of her liturgy, in other words, Christ, God Incarnate, God present among us, and not man or the community.

A lived reality

Benedict XVI approached the liturgy with faith, amazement, deep respect, and a sense of the sacred, making it evident that at the heart of his activity there was a real and true encounter with God, with the Person of Christ. Those who participated in his liturgical celebrations noticed this experience that he had and was capable of transmitting to the thousands of people present in Saint Peter's Basilica or on the squares, in the stadiums, or in the parks. When he celebrated, he made you understand that the encounter taking place at that moment was not with him personally, but with the Person of Christ. All his liturgies, as well as many moments that were not part of the liturgy, always expressed this encounter with Christ. He experienced them with the mind-set that recalls the words of Saint Paul: "For what we preach is not ourselves, but Jesus Christ as Lord, with ourselves as your servants for Jesus' sake" (2 Cor 4:5). We can serenely declare that his work of evangelization was profoundly Theocentric, Christocentric, and Pneumocentric. For Benedict XVI, indeed, the liturgy is also a participation in the prayer of Christ, addressed to the Father in the Holy Spirit; in it, every Christian prayer finds its goal (*CCC* 1073).

The liturgy actualizes and manifests the Church as a visible sign of God's communion with mankind through Christ (*CCC* 1071). Christ at the center of his apostolic activity. Christ at the center of the liturgy. Christ at the center of life.

Directed toward him

In order to underscore this essential centrality for the life of the Church and for the worship of the Lord, Benedict XVI asked that a crucifix be placed at the center of the altar, especially when the liturgy is celebrated on it *versus populum* [facing the people]. He liked to recall that this centrality is an essential part of our life as baptized Christians. "For me, to live is Christ", Saint Paul declares. For at the origin of the act of faith there is an Encounter, adherence to a person, the Person of Christ. Benedict XVI warned us against the danger of forgetting this fundamental, active centrality of the primacy of God, when we celebrate as though he did not exist, as though he were not there, when we celebrate ourselves, when we celebrate the community or the celebrant.

The experience of the postconciliar years plainly showed the damage caused by a self-referential concept of the Church and of the liturgy. On the contrary, the cultic and cultural dimension of the Catholic liturgy is profoundly centered and oriented. It is urgent for us to rediscover this center and this orientation! I think, indeed, that this will be a pressing question that we will have to address and resolve if we do not want to fall into insignificance and to accelerate even more the desertification of our churches and our liturgies, which are already abandoned, especially by young people.

A new generation

Benedict XVI, surprisingly, was capable of attracting young people by making them understand the central character of Christ and of his divine presence in the liturgy. It was a very beautiful testimony to see so many young people praying in silence during Eucharistic adoration at the World Youth Days. Many young priests understood and admired the liturgical teaching of Benedict XVI. They gave a moving testimony of this by participating in his funeral in large numbers.

Benedict XVI attracted because he seemed to want to disappear in the liturgy so that Christ alone might be seen.

During a liturgical celebration, he always spoke gently and sweetly without offending anyone, while giving the reasons to believe and inviting the listeners to an evangelical conversion without conventional moralizing, by placing Christ at the center. People saw Benedict XVI as a person who had let himself be attracted, involved, and transformed by Christ, who is present and gathers us in the liturgy. He is the one who calls us together in the liturgy, in him we are united, and through him we go out into the world to proclaim to our brothers and sisters the Good News of the Kingdom of God and to respond to human needs: "The love of Christ has united us", a French hymn says. For Benedict XVI, this spiritual dimension was part of his everyday life as a Christian, a theologian, and a pastor.

He restored the sacral dimension in the liturgy to its place of honor, opposing some sociologists and theologians who would like to declare that, for postmodern man, definitively, there is no longer any sacred space or sacred character because everything is supposedly sacred. But when everything is sacred, nothing is sacred anymore. That way of thinking opened the doors to the present-day relativism and nihilism, which are destroying humanity and society from within. The people of our time, especially the young ones, need to be reinitiated today into the sacred character of worship and of life. They bear within themselves a profound nostalgia for it, sometimes in a way that is not expressed.

Benedict had started this work with much success. What some adults criticized, the young people admired, especially the priests, religious, and seminarians. As in the case of John Paul II, we can say that an unexpected generation of papal fans was born with Benedict XVI. He led young people in reflecting on complex topics with the simplicity that is typical of great minds, and I am convinced that his legacy will be great for the near future of the Church and that it will even increase. Today, those among the young generations who feel with deep conviction that they are in the Church owe this to John Paul II and to Pope Benedict XVI, who will be more and more present now that he is no longer among us visibly.

III

High Priest and Confessor of the Faith

Preface to
Benoît XVI et le ministère pétrinien,
by Christian Gouyaud

[As I read the pages of the book by Father Christian Gouyaud, *Benedict XVI and the Petrine Ministry*,] a thought came to my mind: not only the teachings, but also the acts and the style of Benedict XVI are a theological topic that must be studied in order to understand better the meaning of the Petrine ministry.

Christian Gouyaud had the innovative insight to make a genuine theological interpretation of this pontificate. He was able to demonstrate its internal consistency and to set forth the fundamental lines of it in a magisterial synthesis. He also showed how Joseph Ratzinger, from the first years of his teaching, elaborated an original concept of the Petrine ministry and of the episcopal office.

I am convinced that Pope Benedict XVI renewed our theological understanding of the supreme pontificate and, thereby, of the episcopacy and the priesthood.

This renewed understanding is rooted in an in-depth reading of Scripture, as the author of *Jesus of Nazareth* taught us to do. Joseph Ratzinger remarks, in fact, that nowadays the verse from the Gospel of Saint Matthew:

"You are Peter, and on this rock I will build my Church" (Mt 16:18) is generally designated as the scriptural foundation for the papal primacy. However, in the early Church, the decisive verse for understanding the primacy of Peter and of his successors, the bishops of Rome, was verse 16, Saint Peter's profession of faith: "You are the Christ, the Son of the living God." [As Father Gouyaud writes,] it is precisely "as bearer of the *Credo* that Peter becomes the rock of the Church, the one responsible for her faith in God, which is faith in Christ as Son and, for that very reason, faith in the Father and a Trinitarian faith that only the Spirit can impart." Hence, for Joseph Ratzinger, verses 17–19 "are only an interpretation of verse 16. For to say the *Credo* is never man's own work."

This profession of faith by Saint Peter occurs in a very particular context. The Evangelist Matthew situates it six days before the Transfiguration (Mt 17:1), which takes place on the day of the Jewish feast of *Sukkot*, the Festival of Booths. This dating allows us to state that Peter's profession of faith took place on the day of *Yom Kippur*, the feast of great forgiveness.[1]

Now, everyone knows that this was the only day of the year on which the high priest, setting foot in the Holy of Holies of the Temple, could utter before the presence of the Most High the proper Name of God, the sacred, unpronounceable tetragrammaton: YHWH. By this ritual, which is inscribed at the heart of the sacrificial liturgy of the Temple, the high priest obtained forgiveness for the sins of the people. Indeed, it renewed the gesture of Moses after the episode of the idolatry of the golden

[1] See Jean-Marie Van Cangh and Michel van Esbroeck, "La Primauté de Pierre et son contexte judaïque", *Revue théologique de Louvain* 11, no. 3 (1980): 310–24.

calf. Observing the breach of the covenant by the people, Moses then went back up the mountain to God. "And the LORD descended in the cloud and stood with him there, and [Moses] proclaimed the name of the LORD" (Ex 34:5).

Thus Saint Peter, by his profession of faith, is at the same time the new high priest and the new Moses. In pronouncing the Name of the Lord before the Incarnate Word: "You are the Son of the living God", he performs in truth a priestly action. Standing before Christ, he is in the true Holy of Holies. He pronounces the name that neither flesh nor blood can inspire in him. He truly performs an act of worship. He renews the liturgy that reconciles man and God. For, like Moses, in pronouncing in God's presence the Divine Name in an act of faith, he provokes the divine response, which is a response of covenant and forgiveness.[2]

Confessing the Divine Name is therefore the distinguishing feature of the Petrine ministry. Confessing the truth about God is the act proper to the Supreme Pontiff. It is very important to understand this in order to grasp that Benedict XVI is not only a great theologian. He is not in the first place an intellectual. He is a confessor of the faith in the primary sense of the word. In affirming the truth of the faith as bishop and as pope, Benedict XVI knows that he is carrying out the very essence of the role of Peter. Confessing the faith is not on the order of academic discourse. It is the renewal of this liturgy of the Temple that obtains forgiveness and restores the covenant broken by sin. It is truly an act of worship and a liturgy.

I think that the strands from which the pontificate of Benedict XVI is woven are formed in this profound

---

[2] See Jean-Miguel Garrigues, *Dieu sans idée du mal*, 3rd ed. (Paris: Éditions Ad Solem, 2016), 117.

understanding of Peter's confession of faith. First, as Father Christian Gouyaud emphasizes, the pope is fundamentally a servant. "He ought to be the guarantor of obedience, so that the Church cannot do whatever she likes. The pope cannot say: 'L'Église, c'est moi' (I am the Church). On the contrary, he is bound by a commitment; he embodies this commitment of the Church. He is a rampart against arbitrariness." For the only reason he is there is to confess the Name in an act that is simultaneously magisterial, cultic, and pastoral. The only reason for the pope's place in the Church is so that, in his turn, he can let the Holy Spirit place upon his lips the truth of God and of Revelation. We can gauge the strength with which Benedict XVI sought to correspond to this vocation! I recall the homilies that he gave in the presence of the Blessed Sacrament in Lourdes or in Rome. They are the contemporary echoes of Peter's words. Before Christ, present in the Eucharist, we heard the words resound once again: "You are the Son of the living God!"

In rereading his encyclicals, we hear everywhere the vibrant act of theological faith of the successor of Peter. These documents are cries of faith. They do not aim to satisfy the intellect of the learned, but rather they tell the faith of the Servant of the Truth. Now, the truth has a name: Jesus. We cannot help recalling here the unforgettable sentence that opens *Deus caritas est*: "Being Christian is not the result of an ethical choice or a lofty idea, but the encounter with an event, a Person, which gives life a new horizon and a decisive direction." Confessing the Name of God allows us to meet him personally, to make a covenant with him. The homilies of Pope Benedict XVI will become part of our breviary someday, I hope. They will retain their freshness with those of the Fathers of the Church, with the sermons of Saint Gregory and Saint Leo, his predecessors on the Chair of Peter. Like Moses, he led us up the mountain to meet God. We have once again experienced a confession of faith pronounced with authority and in the name of all humanity before the living God.

But there is another feature that must be emphasized here. As was said, Peter's confession of faith was pronounced in the context of the feast of *Yom Kippur*. It is consequently a liturgical act of worship. Some have thought that the liturgy was a whim of Pope Benedict XVI, a professorial obsession or a personal taste. I am deeply convinced that that is not at all the case. Father Gouyaud is right to emphasize this aspect as an essential feature of the Petrine ministry in the case of Joseph Ratzinger. To teach the liturgy, to take care of it, to celebrate it diligently, is also to confess the Name of God. It is to carry on, as Supreme Pontiff, with the work of the high priest in the Holy of Holies. Truly, the long struggle of Joseph Ratzinger for the traditional liturgical orientation must be interpreted at this theological and spiritual level. Benedict XVI was this new high priest who leads the people to God. For Joseph Ratzinger, indeed, the liturgy is essentially a profession of faith in the objective presence of God. To transform it into the community's celebration of itself rather than a confession of the one true Name would therefore distort it completely. Accepting the findings of Louis Bouyer [based on the research of E. L. Sukenik], Joseph Ratzinger explains that "the Christian house of God comes into being in complete continuity with the synagogue" [*The Spirit of the Liturgy*, p. 77], which was conceivable only in relation to the Temple. Now, the synagogue was not "a local community [that] has become, so to speak, independent, self-sufficient" [ibid., p. 79]; it was oriented toward Jerusalem. Christians, for their part, no longer turn toward Jerusalem but toward the East: "In the early Church, prayer toward the east was regarded as an apostolic tradition ... and was always regarded as an essential characteristic of Christian liturgy" [ibid. p. 82]. It has a Christological (cf. Ps 19:6) and eschatological significance—"Christ in the symbol of the rising sun is the indication of a Christology defined eschatologically" [ibid., p. 83]; the Lord at his Second Coming will be the final dawn of history. Liturgical orientation is not an aesthetic caprice; it is the prolongation of the liturgy of Peter's confession of faith.

The first Supreme Pontiff did not found the Church. He did not gather the apostles in a circle around him. He proclaimed the faith before the Incarnate Word. This oriented proclamation is what makes Peter the new high priest who leads us on behind him, toward the living God. When Pope Benedict XVI celebrated this way facing the Cross, he renewed Peter's gesture. He proclaimed the truth of the unique Name while facing God. I cannot help remembering here liturgies celebrated in the Sistine Chapel facing the Cross in front of the fresco by Michelangelo. Literally, the whole assembly seemed to follow the high priest in this eschatological procession toward the Last Judgment.

And who can forget the Corpus Christi processions in the streets of Rome? Citing the fact that the tabernacle did not exist in the churches of the first millennium, some scholars thought they had a right to claim that Eucharistic worship outside the Mass was "a deviation of medieval piety that should be done away with once and for all". Joseph Ratzinger shows how slogans such as "The Eucharistic Gifts are for eating, not for looking at" [ibid., p. 99] violently disconnect Communion from adoration. The more in-depth theological understanding of Christ's will to dwell with his people fully justifies the presence of the tabernacle in church buildings: "It is the place of the 'Holy of Holies'. It is the tent of God, his throne. Here he is among us" [ibid., p. 103]. Once again, we hear in these words an echo of Peter's confession of faith. We cannot help quoting here the very recent notes that the pope emeritus gave us on the subject of the scandal of criminal pedophilia: "If we reflect on what should be done, it is clear that we do not need another Church of our own design. Rather, what is necessary is a renewal of faith in the reality of Jesus Christ given to us in the Blessed Sacrament" [*What Is Christianity?* (San Francisco: Ignatius Press, 2023), p. 192].

Finally, I would like to emphasize how for Joseph Ratzinger this twofold role of servant of the truth and high priest led him to make his own the very life of Christ who is the way, the truth, and the life. He thus becomes a "coworker of the truth", as his motto says, in an existential sense; he becomes a coworker in the great work of Christ that is his redemption by the Cross.

I think that it is necessary to emphasize the connection that he establishes between the Truth, the Cross, and martyrdom. This connection between the Truth and the Cross is a fundamental idea of Benedict XVI. He writes in the encyclical *Spe salvi*: "the capacity to suffer for the sake of the truth is the measure of humanity. Yet this capacity to suffer depends on the type and extent of the hope that we bear within us." Indeed, "Does truth matter to me enough to make suffering worthwhile?" The pope adds: "But in truly great trials, where I must make a definitive decision to place the truth before my own welfare, career, and possessions, I need the certitude of that true, great hope of which we have spoken here. For this, too, we need witnesses—martyrs—who have given themselves totally, so as to show us the way—day after day."

Consequently, the depth of Peter's confession of faith logically leads to the acceptance of the Cross and of martyrdom. The Petrine ministry is essentially connected with the Cross and with martyrdom for the Truth. As early as 1977, Joseph Ratzinger [in his essay "The Primacy of the Pope and the Unity of the People of God", in *Church, Ecumenism, and Politics* (San Francisco: Ignatius Press, 2008), 48, citing Reginald Cardinal Pole] thought that "the Chair of the Vicar of Christ is the one that Peter established in Rome when he planted the Cross of Christ there.... During his entire pontificate he never descended from it, but rather, 'exalted with Christ' according to the spirit, his hands and feet were fastened with nails in such a way that he wished, not to go where his own will urged him, but rather to remain wherever God's will guided him." [Father Gouyaud says that] for Benedict XVI, "the primacy developed from the beginning as a primacy of martyrdom." In a context of persecutions during the first three centuries, "the principal task of the See of the Bishop of Rome was to resist these persecutions and to give witness to Christ." The consensus of Church and state is certainly more valuable than conflict. Nevertheless: "The Church, the Christian, and above all the pope must always expect to see the witness that they must give become a scandal, not to be accepted, and that then the pope is put in the situation of the witness, of the suffering Christ." The fact is that "all the early popes" were martyrs: "The pope must not appear as a glorious sovereign; he is there to give witness to the one who was crucified...." Speaking about the papal office, Ratzinger writes [*Church, Ecumenism, and Politics*, pp. 48–49]: "The authentic place of the Vicar of Christ is the Cross: being the Vicar of Christ is abiding in the obedience of the Cross and thus *representatio Christi* in the age of this world, keeping his power present to counterbalance the power of the world."

Joseph Ratzinger's thought renews our theological understanding of the Petrine ministry. He sheds new light

not only on the role of the successor of Peter, but also on
the reality of the episcopate and, therefore, of the pres-
byterate. We can say that the role of the bishop is to confess the true Name by making himself a servant of the
divine truth and high priest of this truth. He must even
go so far as to become a coworker of the truth, in other
words, of Christ, by mounting the Cross, to the point of
martyrdom. The place of bishops is on the Cross. In his
recent notes concerning the abuse of minors, Benedict XVI
emphasized that the word *martyr* comes from procedural
law; it designates someone who gives public testimony.
Peter's confession of faith takes on this sense completely; it
is a testimony in favor of the truth. It constitutes Peter as
a martyr, as a witness to the truth. It gives us the profound
meaning of the episcopate.

I think that this is the reason why Joseph Ratzinger
always fought against the reduction of the role of bishops to
that of an administrator. In *The Ratzinger Report*, Cardinal
Ratzinger pointed out "another of the paradoxical effects
of the post-conciliar period": "The decisive new emphasis
on the role of the bishops is in reality restrained or actually risks being smothered by the insertion of bishops into
episcopal conferences that are ever more organized, often
with burdensome bureaucratic structures." He goes on to
recall that "the episcopal conferences have no theological
basis, they do not belong to the structure of the Church,
as willed by Christ" [p. 59]. For the future pope, the collective must not replace the personal, inalienable responsibility of each bishop, which could easily be diluted in
anonymous committees. An episcopal conference, as such,
has no teaching mission: "its documents have no weight
of their own." Moreover, "the national level is not an
ecclesial dimension" [p. 60]. Some have tried to see these
statements as nervousness about synodality; I think, on the

contrary, that they are instead a sign of real perspicacity in his theological understanding of the episcopate.

Allow me to cite here at length a little-known text[3] by Joseph Ratzinger in which he offers his personal insights into the future of the episcopal ministry:

A theologian friend told me one day with his characteristic bitter humor that bishops today are nothing but "mitered bureaucrats". Even my friend will acknowledge that this opinion is exaggerated. It is true that often the best way to draw attention to a threatening truth is by exaggerating. . . .

The fact is that we have become witnesses to a dissolution of the bishop's personal responsibility into the anonymity of collective decisions, a dissolution for which there is no historical precedent. Just think of the number of hours that a bishop must devote to the most varied committee meetings. . . . When we make this observation, we must recall furthermore that the idea of a council or advisory board assisting the bishop is certainly present in the classic ecclesial tradition. Moreover the monastic tradition has always assigned great importance to council meetings. . . . However, the Code of Canon Law, which defines the cathedral chapter as the bishop's senate and council, indicates as the first purpose of the chapter the liturgical service of God in the Church. This signals a connection for which people often no longer find time because of the increase in administrative tasks. . . .

The general decadence in the Church is not surprising at all if this praying center disappears from the heart of the local Church. Are we not witnessing a reversal of values, when in comparison to indispensable administrative work people think that they can do without the service

[3] The text in question is the very substantial preface to the anthology edited by P. Delhaye and L. Elders, *Episcopale munus: Recueil d'études sur le ministère épiscopal* (Assen: Van Gorcum, 1982), xvii–xxii.

of prayer? A council that truly wants to be a council to build up the Church must be rooted in a community of prayer; otherwise it weakens and becomes an instrument for group strategy. A church which, in essential matters, is founded on such councils, can still erect powerful structures, but it is no longer alive....

What reason does it have left to exist when the service of God (the Divine Office) seems to it to be a waste of time that takes it away from more important works? What can we still expect of a council or a committee that isolates itself for discussions, when in the cathedral across the street one of the solemn Christian feast days is being celebrated? This means that for the bishop himself liturgy and preaching are not secondary in comparison to meetings, receptions, discussions, and the study of administrative documents: they are essential purposes to which he should dedicate the majority of his time in private and in public.

We cannot help but recognize in these words an announcement of what the pontificate of Benedict XVI would be. He was a great liturgist and an exceptional preacher, not as a matter of personal taste, but because he took his episcopal and primatial responsibility seriously. Indeed, Joseph Ratzinger continues, "in our secularized world, we feel ill at ease with the sacred and also with the primacy of worship and prayer. We are tempted to consider them as a way to avoid serving unfortunate people. These two factors are opposed to the figure of the bishop as tradition presents it to us, and they make the exercise of the episcopal ministry difficult." We must take this observation seriously. Certainly it was necessary for the episcopacy to get rid of worldly pomp and ceremony that had become oppressive. But in trying to desacralize the figure of the bishop, the theorists cut him off from the primacy of worship and of the sacred. They transformed bishops into clerical officials, thus creating a genuine identity crisis for many of them who now wonder about the legitimacy of their authority. Some even refuse to govern and tend to hide behind a misunderstood synodality.

In the continuation of the preface under discussion, the future Benedict XVI emphasizes that contemporary democratic culture distrusts the right and duty of an individual human being to make decisions.

> People prefer to trust the majority rather than their own conscience and freedom.... However, what tradition expresses with the term "monarchical episcopate", which sounds rather strange to our ears, means that personal responsibility is an irreplaceable and inalienable element in the structure of the Church. In the final analysis, the institution appears, not in a collective entity, but in a person who personally vouches for it.... This is true above all in relation to the episcopal conference: this would not be progress in the development of the constitutive law of the Church if in fact it reduced the ultimate and personal responsibility of the bishop in his diocese. It is obvious that this danger exists; we must not pretend not to see it, but instead squarely address it. A reduction in the claims of episcopal conferences would also promote an increased presence of the bishop in his diocese with his faithful.

I think that nowadays these arguments have lost none of their urgency. Every bishop must rediscover the meaning of his personal responsibility in God's sight. Every bishop must rediscover the responsibility to proclaim the faith in person, in a magisterial and cultic act. As Joseph Ratzinger says, "a bishop who, on the basis of the faith, makes the sacred central does not have to fear that he will go over people's heads this way." There is no better way of expressing the ontological and necessary connections among the *tria munera* [three offices of governing, teaching, and sanctifying].

As we see, the remarkable work by Father Gouyaud opens the way to many more in-depth studies and touches on a number of burning issues. It is now an indispensable tool for all who would like to work on these questions and allow themselves to be nourished by the witness of Benedict XVI, a martyr of truth. I hope that he finds many readers of this French edition but also in the translations that no doubt will be made of this important book. Once again I thank Father Christian Gouyaud for having highlighted the confession of faith of Benedict XVI, which will support the Universal Church for many years. The book by Father Christian Gouyaud, *Benoît XVI et le ministère pétrinien*, is now an essential summary for anyone who wants to understand in depth the pontificate of Benedict XVI.

IV

Like a Saint Augustine of Modern Times

Article published in the magazine
La Nef, February 2023

Many tributes emphasize how great a theologian Benedict XVI was. There is no doubt about that. His work will endure. His brilliant books are already classics. But make no mistake. His greatness is not primarily in his scholarly penetration of the concepts of theological science, but rather in the theological depth of his contemplation of the divine realities. Benedict XVI had the gift of making us see God through his speech, of making us taste his presence through his words. I think that I can say that every one of the homilies that I heard him pronounce was a genuinely spiritual experience that left its impression on my soul. In this regard, he is a true descendant of Saint Augustine, this Doctor of the Church to whom he felt so close spiritually.

His voice, simultaneously frail and warm, managed to make us aware of the theological experience that he himself had had through his practice of the virtues of faith, hope, and charity. The sound of it came to grasp you by the innermost recesses of the heart so as to lead you into the presence of God. Listen to him: "In our days, when in vast areas of the world the faith is in danger of dying out like a flame that no longer has fuel, the overriding priority is to make God present in this world and to show men and women the way to God. Not just any god, but the God who spoke on Sinai; to that God whose face we recognize in a love that presses 'to the end' (cf. Jn 13:1)—in Jesus Christ, crucified and risen."[1]

Benedict XVI was not a rigid ideologue. He was a lover of the truth, which, for him, was not a concept but a person whom he had met and loved: Jesus, God made man. Recall his magisterial statement: "Being Christian is not the result of an ethical choice or a lofty idea, but the encounter with an event, a person, which gives life a new horizon and a decisive direction."[2] Benedict XVI led us to experience this faith encounter with Christ Jesus. Everywhere he went, he kindled this flame in hearts. When he was with young people, seminarians, priests, heads of state, the poor, and the sick, he revived the joy of faith with strength and discretion. He was self-effacing so as to make the faith that he heralded shine brighter. He used to recall: "Only by having a certain experience can one then understand it." He never stopped reminding us that this experience of encountering Christ contradicts neither reason nor free will. "Christ takes nothing away; he gives everything!"

He was sometimes alone, like a child confronting the world. A prophet of the Truth, who is Christ, confronting the empire of falsehood, a frail messenger confronting special interests and calculating authorities. Confronting the giant Goliath of relativist dogmatism and of all-powerful consumerism, he had no other weapon but speech. This modern-day David dared to challenge his listeners:

[1] Benedict XVI, Letter to the Bishops of the Catholic Church concerning the Remission of the Excommunication of the Four Bishops Consecrated by Archbishop Lefebvre, March 10, 2009.

[2] Benedict XVI, Encyclical *Deus caritas est* (December 25, 2005), no. 1.

The desire for the truth is part of human nature itself. The whole of creation is an immense invitation to seek those responses that open human reason to the great response that it has always sought and awaited: "The truth of Christian Revelation, found in Jesus of Nazareth, enables all men and women to embrace the 'mystery' of their own life. As absolute truth, it summons human beings to be open to the transcendent, while respecting both their autonomy as creatures and their freedom. At this point, the relationship between freedom and truth is complete, and we understand the full meaning of the Lord's words: 'You will know the truth, and the truth will make you free' (Jn 8:32)."[3]

But falsehood and compromise could not tolerate him. Outside the Church, but also within her, forces were unleashed. They caricatured what he said. They distorted and ridiculed it. The world wanted to silence him because his message was unbearable to it. They tried to gag him. Benedict then revived in our time the figure of the popes of antiquity, martyrs who were crushed by the Roman Empire that was in its last throes. The world, like Rome back then, trembled before this old man with the heart of a child. The world had compromised too much with falsehood to dare to listen to the voice of its conscience. Benedict XVI was a martyr for the truth, for Christ. Betrayal, dishonesty, sarcasm—they would spare him nothing. He would experience the mystery of iniquity to the very end.

Then we saw the discreet man fully reveal his soul as a pastor and a father, like a new Saint Augustine. This fatherhood of a pastor displayed the maturity of his holiness. Who could forget that evening when, having gathered

---

[3] Benedict XVI, Address to the Participants of the Plenary Assembly of the Congregation for the Doctrine of the Faith (February 10, 2006), citing *Fides et ratio*, no. 15.

priests from all over the world on Saint Peter's Square, he wept with them, laughed with them, and opened up to them the innermost recesses of his priestly heart? Many young people owe to him their vocation to the priesthood or the religious life. Benedict XVI beamed like a father in the midst of his children when he was surrounded by priests and seminarians. Until the end, he tried to support them and to speak to them from the depths of his heart, which was called to follow Christ in the gift of himself even to the point of suffering for others. "If the gift is not to humiliate the other person, I must give to him not only something belonging to me, but myself. Christ, in suffering for all of us, conferred a new meaning on suffering; he brought it into a new dimension, into a new order: the order of love."

Benedict XVI loved families and the sick. In order to understand him, you have to have seen him visit children in the hospital. You have to have seen him offer a gift to each one. You have to have noticed the discreet tear of emotion that made his kindly eyes shine.

To him, we should remember, we owe the Church's clarity on the subject of crimes of pedophilia. He was able to call sin by its name, to meet and listen to the victims, and to punish the perpetrators without the complicity that sometimes is disguised as mercy.

Despite this, or perhaps because of this love for the truth, he was despised more and more. Then the prophet, the martyr, the kindly father became the master of prayer. I cannot forget that evening in Madrid where in the presence of more than a million enthusiastic young people he set aside the speech that he had prepared so as to invite them to pray in silence with him. You had to see these young people from all over the world, kneeling silently behind the one who set the example for them. That evening, by his silent prayer, he gave birth to a new generation of young Christians: "Only adoration makes us truly free; it alone gives us the criteria for our actions. In a world where criteria and guidelines are missing, where there is the danger that everyone will make himself his own standard, it is fundamentally important to emphasize adoration."

This is the profound reason for his insistence on the importance of the liturgy. He knew that, in the liturgy, the Church finds herself face to face with God. If, in that setting, she is not in her correct place, then she is hastening to her destruction. He often repeated that the crisis in the Church was fundamentally a liturgical crisis, in other words, a loss of the sense of adoration. "The mystery is the heart from which we draw our strength!" he liked to repeat. He worked so hard to restore to Christians a liturgy that is, as he himself put it, "a genuine dialogue of the Son with the Father".

Confronted with a world that was deaf to the truth, sometimes confronted with an ecclesiastical institution that refused to listen to his appeal, Benedict XVI finally chose silence as his last sermon. By resigning from his office, by withdrawing in prayer, he reminded us all that "We need men whose intellects are illumined by the light of God, whose hearts God opens so that their intellect can speak to the intellect of others, and their heart can open the hearts of others." By retiring to Mater Ecclesiae Monastery, in Vatican City, Benedict XVI intended to remind the entire Church and each one of us about the primacy of God, of silent prayer, of meditative study of God's Word, of contemplation and daily adoration of Jesus in the Eucharist. His life with God was the heart of his existence. Without knowing it, the pope thus sketched his own portrait, even adding: "Genuine revolution, a decisive change in the world, comes only from the saints, only from God."

Might Benedict XVI have been the last gleam of Christian civilization? The twilight of an era that is over? Some would like to think so. It is true that, without him, we feel like orphans, deprived of that guiding star. But now his light is in us. Benedict XVI, by his teaching and his example, is the Father of the Church of the third millennium. The joyous, peaceful light of his faith will enlighten us for a long time.

V

A Light in the Darkness:
In the Midst of the Sexual Abuse Crisis,
Benedict XVI's View of the Church

Talk given in Rome at the
Centre Saint-Louis, May 14, 2019

Pope Emeritus Benedict XVI composed some notes in view of the Summit Meeting of the Presidents of Bishops' Conferences on sexual abuse, convoked in Rome by Pope Francis from February 21 to 24 of this year, and published them in a Bavarian review [*Klerusblatt*], with the approval of the Holy Father and of the Cardinal Secretary of State.

Now his reflection has proved to be a genuine source of light in the dark night of faith that is affecting the whole Church. He provoked reactions that sometimes border on intellectual hysteria. I was personally struck by the poor quality and the stupidity of many commentaries. You have to think that once again Ratzinger the theologian, whose stature is that of a true "Father and Doctor of the Church", deployed the nuclear option, aimed accurately, and hit the heart of the crisis in the Church.

My wish this evening, therefore, is that we might let ourselves be enlightened by this demanding, luminous thought. How could we summarize the thesis of Benedict XVI? Allow me simply to quote him: "How could pedophilia reach such proportions? In the final analysis, the reason lies in the absence of God" (III, 1).[1] This is the architectonic principle of the whole reflection by the pope emeritus. This is the conclusion of his long demonstration. This is the point from which all research on the scandal of sexual abuse committed by priests must start in order to propose an effective solution.

The crisis of pedophilia in the Church and the scandalous and frightening multiplication of cases of abuse have one and only one ultimate cause: the absence of God. Benedict XVI sums it up in another formula that is just as clear. I quote: "Such offenses are possible only when faith no longer determines man's actions" (II, 2).

Joseph Ratzinger's theological genius agrees here not only with his experience as a pastor of souls and a bishop, the father of his priests, but also with his personal spiritual and mystical experience. He goes back to the fundamental cause; he helps us to understand the only possible way of getting over the horrible and humiliating scandal of pedophilia. The sexual abuse crisis is the symptom of a deeper crisis: the crisis of the faith, the crisis of the sense of God.

Some commentators, out of spite or incompetence, pretended to think that Benedict was saying that only clerics who deviated doctrinally became child abusers. Clearly he is not making this sort of simplistic generalization. What Pope Ratzinger tries to show and demonstrate is much more profound and radical. He declares that a climate of atheism and of the absence of God creates the moral, spiritual, and human condition for a proliferation of sexual abuse.

[1] References given in parentheses are to the article by Benedict XVI that appeared in the journal *Klerusblatt* on April 10, 2019. English translation from Benedict XVI, *What Is Christianity? The Last Writings* (San Francisco: Ignatius Press, 2023), 177–96.

Psychological explanations certainly are of interest, but they only allow us to pinpoint the fragile individuals who are disposed to act out. Only the absence of God can explain a situation in which cases of abuse proliferate and multiply so horribly.

Now we come to the demonstration by Pope Benedict. First of all, it is advisable to settle the score with the lazy, superficial commentaries that tried to disqualify this theological reflection by accusing it of confusing homosexual behavior and sexual abuse of minors. Nowhere does Benedict XVI say that homosexuality is the cause of abuse. It goes without saying that the overwhelming majority of homosexual persons are not suspected of wanting to abuse anyone. But it is necessary to say that the investigations into the sexual abuse of minors have shown the tragic extent of homosexual practices or simply unchaste behavior within the clergy. And this phenomenon, too, is a painful manifestation, as we will see, of a climate of the absence of God and the loss of faith.

Moreover other readers—whether they were too hasty or too silly, I do not know—charged Benedict XVI with historical ignorance on the pretext that his demonstration begins by mentioning the crisis in 1968. Now, the cases of sexual abuse began before that—obviously—and Benedict XVI knows and affirms it. He intends precisely to show that the moral crisis in 1968 is itself already a manifestation and a symptom of the crisis of faith and not an ultimate cause of it. About this crisis in 1968 he could say: "Such offenses are possible only when faith no longer determines the actions of human beings."

Now let us follow his demonstration step by step. It takes up the first part of his article. He tries to show the deep process that is at work here. He affirms, I emphasize, that this process "was long in preparation" and is still "ongoing".

Here Pope Benedict makes use of an example, the development of moral theology, in order to go back to the source of this crisis. He identifies three stages in the crisis of moral theology.

The first stage is the complete abandonment of the natural law as a foundation of morality with the praiseworthy intention—all things considered—of basing moral theology more on the Bible. This attempt resulted in a failure illustrated by the case of the German moralist Schüller.

It leads inevitably to a second stage, namely, a moral theology "defined exclusively on the basis of the purposes of human action" (I, 2). We recognize here the teleological[2] current of which consequentialism was the most dramatic illustration. This current, which is characterized by ignorance of the notion of "moral object", ends up affirming that, as Benedict XVI himself puts it: "There could no longer be anything absolutely good, much less anything categorically evil, but only relative value judgments. There was no longer the good, but only what was relatively better at the moment and depending on the circumstances" (I, 2).

Finally, the third stage is the statement that the Magisterium of the Church is not competent in matters of morality. The Church can teach infallibly only about questions of faith. Nevertheless, as Benedict XVI says, "there is a moral minimum that is inseparably linked to the fundamental decision of faith." Rejection of the Church's moral Magisterium completely disconnects the faith from everyday life. Ultimately, therefore, the faith is indeed emptied of its meaning and reality.

I would like to emphasize that, from the beginning of this process, the absence of God is at work. As early as the first stage, the rejection of the natural law shows that God is forgotten. Indeed, nature is God's first gift. It is in a way

[2] See John Paul II, Encyclical *Veritatis splendor* (August 6, 1993), nos. 74–75.

the first revelation of the Creator. To reject the natural law as a foundation of morality and to pit it against the Bible displays an intellectual and spiritual process that is already at work in this mentality: man's refusal to receive from God the gift of being and the laws of being that manifest its coherence.

The nature of things, Benedict XVI says, is "a wondrous work of the Creator containing a 'grammar' that sets forth ends and criteria".[3] "Man, too, has a nature that he must respect and that he cannot manipulate at will. Man is not merely self-creating freedom. Man does not create himself. He is intellect and will, but he is also nature, and his will is rightly ordered if he respects his nature, listens to it, and accepts himself for who he is, as one who did not create himself."[4] To discover nature as wisdom, order, and law is tantamount to meeting the author of this order. "Is it really pointless to wonder whether the objective reason that manifests itself in nature does not presuppose a creative reason, a *Creator Spiritus*?" Benedict XVI also asked.[5]

I agree with Joseph Ratzinger that the rejection of this Creator-God has long since crept into the heart of Western man. This rejection of God has been at work since well before the crisis in 1968.

But with Pope Benedict we have to show all the successive manifestations of it. The rejection of nature as a divine gift leaves the individual human being desperately alone. From now on, only his subjective intentions and his solitary conscience count. Morality is reduced to the search to understand the motives and the intentions of individuals. It can no longer guide them toward happiness according

---

[3] Benedict XVI, Encyclical *Caritas in veritate* (June 29, 2009), no. 48.

[4] Benedict XVI, Address to the German *Bundestag*, Berlin (September 22, 2011).

[5] Ibid.

to an objective natural order that allows man to discover good and to avoid evil. The rejection of the natural law leads inevitably to the rejection of the notion of the moral object. Hence there are no longer any acts that are always and everywhere objectively and intrinsically bad, whatever the circumstances may be.

Confronted with such thinking, Saint John Paul II intended to recall the objective character of the good in *Veritatis splendor*.[6] Benedict XVI hints that this magisterial encyclical was a work of collaboration between the saintly Polish pope and himself, but also a large number of collaborators who cannot be reduced to a particular school of theology.

Veritatis splendor can therefore declare forcefully that there are acts that are "intrinsically evil,... always and per se, on account of their very object, and quite apart from the ulterior intentions of the one acting and the circumstances" (no. 80), and that this is true because these acts "radically contradict the good of the person".

I would like to emphasize with Benedict XVI that this statement is only the consequence of the objective character of the faith and ultimately of the objectivity of God's existence. If God exists, if he is not merely a creation of my subjectivity, then as the pope emeritus says, "There are values that can never legitimately be sacrificed" (II, 2). For relativist morality, everything becomes a question of circumstances. It is never necessary to sacrifice one's life for God's truth; martyrdom is useless. On the contrary, Benedict XVI affirms that "Martyrdom is a fundamental category of Christian existence. Basically it is no longer morally necessary, in the theory advocated by Böckle and many others, and this shows that the very essence of

[6] See John Paul II, *Veritatis splendor*, nos. 78–83.

Christianity is at stake in this dispute" (I, 2). To sum it up in a few words: If no value is so objective that one must die for it, then the reason is because God himself is no longer an objective reality that is worth the trouble of martyrdom.

At the heart of the crisis of moral theology, therefore, there is a rejection of the divine absolute, of the intervention in our lives of God who surpasses everything, who rules everything, who governs our way of life.[7] The proof by Benedict XVI is clear and definitive; it can be summed up in Dostoyevsky's words: "If God does not exist, then everything is permitted!" If the objectivity of the divine absolute is called into question, then the most unnatural transgressions are possible, even the sexual abuse of a minor. Incidentally, the ideology of 1968 sometimes tried to make society admit the legitimacy of pedophilia. We still have at hand the documents of those libertarian heroes who boasted about their transgressive love affairs with minors. If every moral act becomes relative to the acting subject's intentions and the circumstances, then nothing is definitively impossible and radically contrary to human dignity. The moral atmosphere of the rejection of God, the spiritual climate of the rejection of divine objectivity, is what makes possible the proliferation of the abuse of minors and the trivialization of unchaste acts among clerics.

---

[7] "The Christian faith ... is not the product of our own experiences; rather, it is an event that comes to us from without. Faith is based on our meeting something (or someone) for which our capacity for experiencing things is inadequate.... Certainly, what touches us there effects an experience in us, but experience as the result of an event, not of reaching deeper into ourselves. This is exactly what is meant by the concept of revelation: something not ours, not to be found in what we have, comes to me and takes me out of myself, above myself, creates something new." Joseph Ratzinger, *Truth and Tolerance*, trans. Henry Taylor (San Francisco: Ignatius Press, 2004), 87–89.

As Benedict XVI puts it: "A world without God can be nothing but a world without meaning. Indeed, where does everything that exists come from?... [The world] would somehow exist, and that is all, and it would be devoid of any purpose and meaning. Then there would no longer be any criteria of good or evil. Therefore might would make right, and nothing else. Power then becomes the only principle. Truth does not matter; in reality it does not even exist" (II, 1). If God is not the principle, if truth does not exist, then only power matters. What then is to prevent an adult from abusing that power over a minor? The demonstration by Benedict XVI is clear: "In the final analysis, the reason [for cases of sexual abuse] lies in the absence of God"; "such offenses are possible only when faith no longer determines man's actions."

After establishing this principle, the pope emeritus shows the consequences of it. I personally was very touched by the fact that, in his view, the first consequence is manifested in "the question of priestly life" (II, 1) and the formation of seminarians. Thus it reassures me in one of the fundamental insights of my most recent book.[8]

Benedict XVI writes: "In the context of the meeting of episcopal conference presidents from across the world with Pope Francis [February 21–24, 2019, at the Vatican], the question of priestly life and seminary formation is especially crucial." He points out here the immediate consequence of forgetting God: the crisis of the priesthood. We can say that priests are the first ones affected and that they have taken the Christian people with them. The sexual abuse crisis is the particularly revolting point that has emerged from a profound crisis in the priesthood.

[8] Robert Cardinal Sarah, *For Eternity: Meditations on the Priesthood*, trans. Michael J. Miller (Irondale, Ala.: EWTN Publishing, 2023).

What does it consist of? We will repeat here the exact words of the pope emeritus. For a long time we have seen the spread of a kind of "priestly life" that is no longer "determined" by the faith. Now, if there is one kind of life that should be entirely and absolutely determined by the faith, it is the priestly life. It is and must be a consecrated life, that is, one that is given, reserved, and offered to God alone. Now, very often, we have seen some priests live as though God did not exist.

Here Benedict XVI repeats the words of the theologian von Balthasar: "Do not presuppose [the Triune God]" (III, 1). In other words, do not make him an abstract notion. On the contrary, as Pope Benedict puts it, "Above all, we ourselves must learn again to acknowledge God as the foundation of our life instead of leaving him aside as though he were some empty cliché" (III, 1).

"The subject 'God' seems so unreal, so far removed from the things that concern us." Basically, with these words, Benedict XVI is describing a secularized, profane priestly lifestyle. A life in which God is of secondary importance. He gives some illustrations of it. Some, he says, have claimed that the first concern of the bishops should no longer be God himself but rather "a new, radically open relationship with the world" (II, 1). They transformed the seminaries so as to make them secularized places where, Benedict XVI says, "the climate ... could not foster priestly formation." Indeed, the life of prayer and adoration was neglected there, and the meaning of consecration to God was forgotten. The pope emeritus lists the symptoms of this forgetfulness: mingling with the lay world, which introduces noise into the seminary and denies the fact that every priest, because of his priesthood, is a man separated from the world, set apart for God (II, 1). He mentions also the establishment of homosexual cliques

in the seminaries. This fact is not so much the cause of forgetfulness of God but rather the sign that it has already set-
tled in to a great extent. Indeed, seminarians who openly
live in contradiction with natural and revealed morality
show that they are not living for God. God is no longer the
center of their lives. Maybe they are looking for a profession, maybe they appreciate the social aspects of ministry.
But they have forgotten the essential thing: a priest is a man
of God, a man for God, a man totally belonging to God.

The most serious thing is perhaps that the formators
said nothing. As if the bishops and those responsible for
seminary formation had also renounced the centrality of
God. As if they, too, had relegated the faith to secondary status, thus making it ineffective. As if they, too, had
replaced the primacy of a life for God and according to
God with the dogma of openness to the world, relativism,
and subjectivism. It is striking to see that the objectivity
of God has been eclipsed, so to speak, by a form of religion of human subjectivity. Pope Francis rightly speaks
of self-referentiality. I think that the worst form of self-
referentiality is the kind that denies the reference to God,
to his objectivity, so as to keep only the reference to man
in his subjectivity.

In a climate like that, how can anyone live an authentically priestly life? How can anyone set limits on the temptation to be all-powerful? A man who has only himself as his
point of reference, who lives not for God but for himself,
not according to God but according to his own desires,
will end up falling into the logic of the abuse of power and
of sexual abuse. Who will rein in his desires, even the most
perverse, if his subjectivity is the only thing that matters?
Forgetfulness of God opens the door to all sorts of abuses.
We had already observed this in society. But forgetfulness
of God made its way into the Church, too, and even into

the clergy. Inevitably the abuse of authority and cases of sexual abuse spread among priests.

Practical atheism prepares the ground for the psychology of an abuser. For a long time now the Church has allowed herself to be invaded by this fluid atheism. She should not be surprised to discover abusers and perverts among her members. If God does not exist, everything is permitted! If God does not exist concretely, everything is possible!

In this regard, I would like to emphasize the fine reflection by Pope Benedict concerning canon law in general and penal law in particular.

Indeed, canon law is basically a structure designed to protect the objectivity of our relationship with God. As Benedict XVI emphasizes, the law "must also protect the faith, which likewise is an important good" (II, 2). The faith is our first common good. Through it we become children of the Church. It is an objective good, and the first duty of the authority is to defend it. Now, as the pope emeritus remarks, "In the current understanding of right and wrong, the faith no longer seems to have the status of a good to be protected. This", he emphasizes, "is an alarming situation that the pastors of the Church must bear in mind and take seriously" (II, 2).

This point is of capital importance. The sexual abuse crisis has revealed a crisis of the objectivity of the faith that is manifested also at the level of authority in the Church. Indeed, just as the shepherds refused to punish clerics who teach doctrines contrary to the objectivity of the faith, so too they refuse to punish the clerics guilty of unchaste practices or even cases of sexual abuse. It is the same logic. This is a falsified expression of "garantismo", which Pope Benedict defines as follows: "This means that above all else the rights of the accused had to be guaranteed, to the point where conviction was excluded in practice" (II, 2).

Here we find again the same ideology. The individual subject, his desires, his subjective intentions, the circumstances become the only reality. The objectivity of the faith and of morality becomes secondary. Such an idolatry of the individual subject excludes in fact any penalty or punishment, both for the heretical theologians and for the abusive clerics. By refusing to consider the objectivity of the acts, as Benedict XVI remarks, they abandon the "little ones" and the weak to the delirium of their all-powerful executioners. Yes, through a so-called mercy, they have abandoned the faith of the weak and the little ones. They have left them in the hands of the intellectuals who rejoiced at the thought of deconstructing the faith by their foggy theories that the authorities have refused to condemn. In the same way, they abandoned the victims of sexual abuse. They neglected to condemn the abusers, the executioners of the children's innocence and purity, and sometimes of seminarians or nuns. All this under the pretext of understanding individual subjects, of rejecting the objectivity of the faith and morals. I think that to condemn and to inflict a punishment, both in the order of faith and in the order of morality, is proof of great mercy on the part of the authority.

As Benedict XVI emphasizes, sexual abuse is objectively a "major offense against the faith". To describe it in this way, he says, is "not a ploy so as to be able to impose the maximum penalty, but rather a consequence of the gravity of the faith for the Church. Indeed, it is important to keep in mind that such crimes by clerics ultimately damage the faith" (II, 2).

I think that the real clericalism is the attitude of clerics who have a sense of impunity and toy either with the faith of believers or with their moral life. Yes, clericalism is this attitude of rejecting penalties and punishments in the case of sins against faith and morals. Clericalism is the rejection by clerics of the objectivity of the faith and of morality. The clericalism that Pope Francis calls us to eradicate consists, definitively, in this impenitent subjectivism of clerics!

I still have to address one last consequence of forgetfulness of God and of the objectivity of the faith. If faith no longer shapes our behavior, then the Church is for us, not a divine reality that is received as a gift, but a reality to be constructed according to our ideas and our agenda. I was profoundly shocked and hurt by the reception that some gave to the document by Benedict XVI. Some said, "No one can hear this message", in other words, it is not what the Church needs in order to be credible again.

The Church does not need communications experts. She is not an NGO (non-governmental organization) in crisis that needs to regain its popularity! Her legitimacy is not found in opinion polls; it is in God!

As Benedict XVI puts it: "The crisis caused by the many cases of clerical abuse drives us to regard the Church as a failure, which we must now decisively take into our own hands and redesign from the ground up. However, a Church that we build can offer no hope." As the pope emeritus emphasizes, we see an increase in cases of sexual abuse today precisely because we gave in to the temptation to make the Church in our own image and set God aside. Let us not fall into the same trap again! These cases of abuse reveal a Church that men decided to take into their own hands! I am therefore deeply saddened when I read an article penned by a female theologian saying that the Church has made herself guilty of a "collective sin" or that the Church contributes to a "structure of sin". The same Dominican nun advocates calling into question "the concept of truth" that is the characteristic feature of the Catholic Church. In her opinion, the Church would have to renounce any "claim to expertise or excellence in matters of holiness, truth, and morality".[9]

This kind of approach only leads to sheer subjectivism. It therefore brings us right back to the same cause that produced the crisis. For if truth and morality are no longer taught, then who will be able to maintain that there are things that can never be done? Once again, if God does not exist objectively, if the truth is not imperative, then everything is permitted!

What, then, is the path that Benedict XVI proposes to us? It is simple. If the cause of the crisis is forgetfulness of God, then let us put God back at the center! Let us put back at the center of the Church and of our liturgies the presence of God, his objective and real presence. As prefect of the Congregation for Divine Worship, I was particularly touched by one remark by Benedict XVI. He states that "In conversations with victims of pedophilia, [he had] become more and more acutely aware of this necessity [a renewal of faith in the reality of Jesus Christ given to us in the Blessed Sacrament]" and a renewed, more reverent celebration of the Eucharist (III, 2).

I want to emphasize that this is not a conclusion by some expert in theology but rather the wise word of a pastor who had allowed himself to be touched profoundly by the stories of victims of pedophilia. With his profound tact, Benedict XVI understood that respect for the pure, innocent bodies of children depends on respect for the Eucharistic Body of the Lord.

"The Eucharist [has been] degraded", he says. A way of treating the Blessed Sacrament has appeared "that destroys

---

[9] See Véronique Margron, *Un Moment de vérité* (Paris: Albin Michel, 2019), 65–69, 149.

the greatness of the Mystery". Together with the pope emeritus, I am deeply convinced that unless we adore the Eucharistic Body of our God, unless we treat it with a joyful and reverential fear, then the temptation to profane the bodies of children will spring up among us.

I underscore the conclusion reached by Benedict XVI: "If we reflect on what should be done, it is clear that we do not need another Church of our own design. Rather, what is necessary is a renewal of faith in the reality of Jesus Christ given to us in the Blessed Sacrament" (III, 2).

To conclude, I say again with Pope Benedict: Yes, the Church is full of sinners. But she is not in crisis; we are the ones in crisis. The devil tries to make us doubt. He tries to make us think that God is abandoning his Church. But she is "still God's field.... There will be not only the weeds ... but also God's sowing.... Forcefully proclaiming both proportionately is not false apologetics, but a necessary service to the truth", Benedict XVI says. He proves it; his praying, teaching presence in the midst of us, at the heart of the Church, in Rome, confirms it for us. Yes, there are among us good divine harvests.

Dear Pope Benedict, thank you for being, as your motto says, a coworker, a servant of the truth. Your words strengthen and reassure us. You are a "witness", a "martyr" of the truth.

VI

The African Continent, Spiritual "Lung" of Humanity

Excerpt from an article published in
30 Giorni for the Apostolic Journey
to Benin, October 2011

Africa really was very honored by the pastoral visits of the Holy Father, Pope Benedict XVI, who aimed to encourage the African continent to take its own destiny in hand responsibly and also to reassure it in the midst of its many trials, to strengthen the faith of the Christians, and to awaken the Church to her missionary task. Africa is totally open to Christ. It has made a great leap toward Christ Jesus. In 1900, there were only two million Catholics in all of Africa. Today, they number 147,000,000, with an impressive crop of vocations to the priestly and religious life and many conversions to Christianity. But some vast regions still do not know "the gospel of God" (Mk 1:14).

The first synod on "The Church in Africa and Her Evangelizing Mission" and the second synod about this continent on "The Church in Africa, at the Service of Reconciliation, Justice, and Peace", addressed very seriously and with great commitment the basic questions that concern and torment the whole Church and the African populations: evangelization, inculturation, the Church-Family of God, dialogue as "the way to be Christian within one's community, as well as with other believers", peace and justice, reconciliation, and the massive and powerful influence of the mass media in the cultural, anthropological, ethical, and religious development of our societies. These important questions were studied and discussed in an atmosphere of faith and prayer, examined in humble obedience to the Word of God and under the ever-shining lights of the Spirit who accompanies us throughout history.

I have confidence that with patience, determination, the strength of faith, and God's help, the African continent will know peace, reconciliation, and greater social justice and will be able to contribute to the rediscovery of human, religious, and ethical values: the sacredness of life and respect for it, from conception to natural death; the greatness of marriage between a man and a woman; the meaning and the nobility of the family, which modern societies—especially the Western ones that are morally enfeebled by the "silent apostasy"—"deconstruct" and make vague and frivolous. It will help to rediscover God, the sense of the sacred, and the reality of sin, in its individual and collective forms.

In addition to its fabulous natural resources, the African continent possesses an extraordinary human wealth. Its population is young and constantly growing. Africa is a fertile field for human life. Unfortunately, despite its natural and human riches, it is tragically affected by poverty and by political and economic instability and disorder. It still experiences the effects of domination, contempt, and colonialism, a phenomenon that apparently is finished on the political level and yet has not ended; it is subtler and more dominating than ever. Because of Africa's technological, economic, and financial weaknesses, the powerful and the shrewd experts of the economic world have

organized the anarchic pillage and exploitation of its natural riches, without any benefit for its populations. Africa
is poor and without money, but it buys weapons with its
natural resources in order to wage wars fomented with the
complicity of certain corrupt, shady African leaders who
could not care less about the atrocious sufferings of the
populations, which are constantly displaced and in flight
from violence, bloody combat, and insecurity.

It is necessary to thank God, however. Today Africa,
as a whole, seems to be experiencing a certain calm in
comparison to the bitter tensions that have left their mark
on the continent in the last two decades. Even though the
peace and security of the populations are still at risk and
fragile in some places, a real development toward pacifi-
cation is evident. With war over—or almost—now it is
necessary to set out on the path toward reconciliation. The
second Synod on Africa arrived at the right moment to
remind Christians that they should be makers of peace and
reconciliation. In order to help the continent to confront
this immense challenge and this difficult battle against poverty and for economic development, for a more humanly
dignified, happier existence, in which the Church should
collaborate with other institutions, the Holy Father, Pope
Benedict XVI, is returning to Africa in order to reassure
Africans of his confidence in their ability to emerge, by
themselves, from this long, painful socioeconomic and
political crisis, through work, unity, and the meeting of
minds, and to remind the Christians in Africa that God has
reconciled us with himself through Christ and has entrusted
to us the ministry of reconciliation (2 Cor 5:18). The Holy
Father will stimulate the energies of the African continent
and, like a father, urge Africans to leave their reserva-
tion and to enter into the major global circles so as to assert
themselves and to demonstrate publicly the cultural values

and the inestimable human and spiritual qualities that they can offer to the Church and to all humanity.

Certainly, today the far greater part of Africa is outside of the major global circles. It is easily left aside and marginalized. Africa is a negligible link in the global chain, facing a world that is totally controlled by the rich and powerful nations, economically, technologically, and militarily. All the armies of the Western countries are deployed almost in their totality in the poor nations of Asia and Africa, bombing and destroying buildings, thousands and thousands of innocent human lives, in order to keep the peace, as they say, and to promote democracy. Iraq and its population are destroyed, and Saddam Hussein was removed. Bin Laden was killed and thrown into the sea. Muammar Gaddafi has just been removed with several members of his family, and they made sure that the memory of him would disappear into the desert sands. Côte d'Ivoire was an economically well-off country. Today it is broken in two and destroyed.... I do not approve of those men and their deeds, which were certainly atrocious and deserved condemnation. But the fact that civilized powers should form a coalition and treat in this way human beings who were created in God's image is barbarous and unforgivable. And if those figures were bandits and dictators to their peoples, why should anyone fear that their tombs might become places of pilgrimage? Maybe other heads of state expect the same fate!

I do not know what God, in his silence, thinks about so much cruelty. His heart is probably very sad. Please forgive this digression. Money and power must no longer be set up as the gods of the world, with human lives offered to them in sacrifice. The truth ought to triumph. God alone is the first and supreme truth. Without the truth, man cannot grasp the meaning of life; then he leaves the field wide open for those who are strongest.[1] The law of "might makes right", violence, and the wars in the world are a major issue and the great wound suffered by mankind today!

The African continent is forgotten by men, but not by God, who manifestly favors the little ones, the poor, and the weak. Pope John Paul II already said in 1995 that

> contemporary Africa can be compared to the man who went down from Jerusalem to Jericho; he fell among robbers who stripped him, beat him, and departed, leaving him half dead (cf. Lk 10:30–37). Africa is a continent where countless human beings—men and women, children and young people—are lying, as it were, on the edge of the road, sick, injured, disabled, marginalized, and abandoned. They are in dire need of Good Samaritans who will come to their aid.[2]

This is why, fortified by their faith in Jesus Christ, the bishops of Africa entrusted their continent to Christ the Lord, the true Good Samaritan, convinced that he alone, through his Gospel and through his Church, can save Africa from its current difficulties and heal it of its many ills. Jesus Christ, his Gospel, and his Church are the hope of Africa, and Africa is the future of the world. Recent popes think so, as I interpret their words. And I think that their view deserves credit, because they expressed themselves this way in the context of their prophetic office and within liturgical celebrations. Their words were not pronounced during a press conference, but in the presence of God and at the heart of the liturgy.

[1] See Benedict XVI, *Jesus of Nazareth: From the Entrance into Jerusalem to the Resurrection* (San Francisco: Ignatius Press, 2011).

[2] John Paul II, Apostolic Exhortation *Ecclesia in Africa* (September 14, 1995), no. 41.

In the Old Testament, the mission of the prophets was to read, interpret, and comment on the history and sociopolitical and religious events, not only of the people of Israel, but also of the peoples who were Israel's neighbors. It is certain that today the popes, the successors of Peter, follow this specific prophetic ministry in order to read, analyze, and interpret Church history and the human, religious, and sociopolitical situations in the world.

And what do the recent popes say about Africa? They clearly express what Africa is in God's eyes and its present and future mission in the world.

Thus Paul VI declared in Kampala in July 1969: "*Nova Patria Christi, Africa.* Christ's new homeland is Africa." God has always paid special attention to Africa, making it collaborate in the salvation of the world. "In fact it was the African continent that welcomed the Savior of the world when the infant Jesus had to flee to Egypt with Mary and Joseph in order to keep his life safe from Herod's persecutions", said His Holiness Benedict XVI. And then it was an African, a certain Simon, originally from Cyrene, the father of Alexander and Rufus, who helped Jesus to carry the Cross (see Mk 15:21).

In 1995, Pope Saint John Paul II wrote in *Ecclesia in Africa*: "'I have written your names on the palms of my hands' (Is 49:15–16). Yes, on the palms of Christ, pierced by the nails of the Crucifixion. The names of each one of you [Africans] is written on those palms."[3]

And Benedict XVI, in his homily for the Opening of the Second Special Assembly for Africa of the Synod of Bishops, on October 4, 2009, said:

Africa is the depository of a priceless treasure for the whole world: its profound sense of God.... Africa constitutes an

[3] Ibid., no. 143.

immense spiritual "lung" for a humanity that appears to be in a crisis of faith and hope. But this "lung" can also become ill. And at this moment at least two dangerous pathologies are infecting it: in the first place, a disease that is already widespread in the Western world, in other words practical materialism, combined with relativist and nihilistic thought.

Hence the importance and the urgency of a deeper evangelization of African mentalities, customs, and cultures, an intense work of deepening and appropriating the faith and the Christian mysteries. The formation of the heart, enabling human persons to establish ties of intimate friendship with Jesus and promoting an intense life of prayer and frequent personal encounters with God, should be promoted and strengthened. In order to achieve this, we have the help, the support, and encouragement of African models of holiness that we are called to imitate: Saint Charles Lwanga and his companion martyrs, Blessed Cyprian Michael Tansi, Saint Josephine Bakhita, Saint Marie-Clémentine Anuarite, martyr, and many others.

VII

Benedict the Great

Preface to
L'Homme qui ne voulait pas être pape,
by Nicolas Diat

Is the papacy of Benedict XVI the story of a missed appointment? Or a wasted opportunity? Or a disappointed hope? In closing the fine book by Mr. Nicolas Diat, *The Man Who Did Not Want to Be Pope*, the reader cannot help being overcome by a feeling of sadness. We are like the apostles on the evening of Holy Saturday. We followed Benedict XVI, the man who did not want to be pope. We listened to him with amazement, we hoped with him, and now suddenly it all seems to stop, buried in silence. Really, like the apostles after Christ's burial, we feel that we are orphans, helpless, without direction or guidance. Here we are, sitting at the side of the road, crushed by the mystery of evil. However, an attentive reading of this book, a reading that is illumined by the faith, should make us go farther.

Some will say that we had as our pope a theologian whose teachings will remain, for many years, as a lighthouse in the night. That is true, but it is quite insufficient. Of course the homilies of Benedict XVI will never be outmoded, since they are so imbued with the essential things. They will always keep their style, forcefulness, and depth, which earn them a place in the tradition of the great homilies of the Fathers of the Church. Benedict XVI is a major theologian; everyone agrees about that. But we must enter more deeply into the mystery of Benedict XVI. He is not just a professor who teaches a doctrine in an altogether external way.

Why, then, did the words of Benedict XVI echo so forcefully in so many hearts and souls? Certainly, Joseph Ratzinger is an intellectual genius, but beyond that, the Word in his communications became profoundly priestly, rooted in the Word of the one High Priest with whom he associated diligently. How could anyone miss in his voice an echo of Christ's voice teaching along the roads of Galilee? His faint, discreet, and timid voice, his unassuming speeches without rhetorical effects shook the world. Recall his very beautiful meditation before the Blessed Sacrament at the foot of the grotto in Lourdes, his very fatherly words to the priests gathered in Saint Peter's Square for the Year of the Priest, his magisterial speeches at the Collège des Bernardins in Paris, in the Bundestag in Berlin, or else his commentaries on Scripture with the seminarians.

Each time, those in attendance went away transformed, moved. What had happened? His speech had become an event, an experience. To listen to Benedict XVI was to have the experience of an encounter with God; it was to let oneself be led, as Saint Augustine says, to love God by God. Since the Holy Spirit is God, we love God by God.[1]

In a very beautiful homily, which for a long time was unpublished, the young Joseph Ratzinger inquired about the place of the word in the life of a priest:

---

[1] Augustine, *Enarrationes in Psalmos*, 140 (*PL* 38:210–13).

Let us begin with the *Word*. We may be inclined to say: "The Word? What is that? Only facts matter; words are nothing." But if you reflect a bit, you come to realize that words have power to create facts. Thus a single lying word can destroy a whole life and sully a person's name irreparably. A single word of kindness can transform a person when nothing else is of any use. It should be clear to us, therefore, how important it is for mankind that there be talk about more than money and war, power and profit, that beyond the babble of everyday life someone should speak about God.... A world that lacks such words becomes infinitely boring and empty. It becomes cheerless.... It is difficult to proclaim God's Word today in a world that is sated with every kind of sensation. It is difficult to proclaim God's Word today in a world in which the priest himself must grope his way with difficulty through the darkness and must choose between saying what no one will understand or, in a hesitant and inadequate way, translating for our world what is so far removed from our everyday experience. The service of the Word has become difficult.... [On many occasions the priest] would have liked to cast away the word that had turned him into a solitary, a fool, a marked man with whom no one wanted to have any dealings. But he had to carry the burden of the word. And precisely by doing so, he served the very people who refused to understand him.[2]

In addressing the young priest who was celebrating his first Mass that day, Joseph Ratzinger prophetically sketched the portrait of the future Benedict XVI! He was this echo of the Word made flesh, this echo of the Logos. Truly his word would "create facts", as the expression goes.

[2] Joseph Ratzinger, "Meditation on the Day of a First Mass", in *Dogma and Preaching*, trans. Michael J. Miller and Matthew J. O'Connell (San Francisco: Ignatius Press, 2011), 369–75.

This experience remains unforgettable for each one of us. By his word, Benedict XVI initiated the whole Church into an experience: the Word of God was addressed to us, and it resounds for us today. Assembled around her Shepherd, the Church repeated the experience of the disciples gathered around Jesus on the mount of the Beatitudes. "In the humility that is also lived in ecclesiality, [there] is an experience of God which is loftier than that attained by reflection. In it we really touch God's Heart."[3] This is the experience to which good Pope Benedict led the whole Church through his word. The Shepherd led his flock until they encountered Christ. Recall the first, very decisive words of the encyclical *Deus caritas est*: "Being Christian is not the result of an ethical choice or a lofty idea, but the encounter with an event, a person, which gives life a new horizon and a decisive direction."[4]

With his beaming goodness, Benedict XVI took us by the hand to lead us to this personal encounter. How did he proceed? He himself tells us: "One encounters the risen Christ in the word and in the sacrament; worship is the way in which he becomes touchable to us and recognized as the living Christ."[5] Truly, he makes us taste the joy of the encounter with the Living Christ at the heart of the liturgy.

This is certainly one of the summits of the pastoral and teaching activity of Pope Benedict. Rather than teach about the liturgy, he celebrated it! Thanks to him, pontifical liturgies became genuine places of theology and magisterial teaching. Perfectly in the spirit of the council, Saint

---

[3] Benedict XVI, General Audience (May 14, 2008).

[4] Benedict XVI, *Deus caritas est* (December 25, 2005), no. 1.

[5] Joseph Ratzinger, *Introduction to Christianity*, trans. J. R. Foster (San Francisco: Ignatius Press, 2004), 309.

Peter's Basilica became the place where the ecclesiology of the council was actually implemented. In the liturgies of Pope Benedict, the Church understood better who she was because she had an experience of God. "Only if there is a certain experience can one also understand."[6]

By reconciling the liturgy with itself, with its history and its tradition, Benedict XVI enabled us to rediscover the taste for God and his central place in our lives. Truly we had an experience of God's beauty and of his grandeur. Who among us did not feel this joyful fear, this humble and jubilant gift of self while participating in the liturgies in Saint Peter's Basilica? We literally felt the extent to which the liturgy "bears within it the fruit of the experience of faith of all preceding generations. Even though the participants do not understand all the words, they perceive their deep significance, the presence of the mystery that transcends all speech."[7]

Down through the centuries, Benedict XVI will remain the pope-liturgist par excellence. Through his teaching, through his liturgical Magisterium, and especially the Motu Proprio *Summorum pontificum*, Pope Benedict profoundly renewed the liturgical sense of Christians. He indicated the direction in which it was necessary to continue the work of the council. "The liturgy of the Church has been for me ... the central reality of my life, ... the center of my theological efforts",[8] he wrote. This theology is not a rational reflection. It is an experience of God in action. The mere recollection of the celebrant Joseph Ratzinger was quite striking. When he displayed at the

[6] Benedict XVI, Address to the Clergy of Rome (February 22, 2007).

[7] Joseph Ratzinger, "The New Evangelization" (address, Convention of Catechists and Religion Teachers, Vatican City, December 10, 2000).

[8] Joseph Ratzinger, preface to *Collected Works*, vol. 11, *Theology of the Liturgy* (San Francisco: Ignatius Press, 2014), xvi (dated June 29, 2008).

altar a humble, attentive *ars celebrandi* [manner of cele-
brating], the joy of his soul became palpable for all the
participants. Everyone found his place in the great family
of the Church.

Someone told me about the case of a person who had
broken with the Catholic Church: after participating in a
Mass on Saint Peter's Square, he quite simply exclaimed,
"That is the Church!" and returned to full communion
with her.

Benedict-the-liturgist, by reconciling the liturgy with
itself, reconciled the Church with herself. Motivated by
the certainty that "the true renewal of the liturgy is a fundamental prerequisite for the renewal of the Church",[9]
Benedict XVI acted very concretely, very simply: he celebrated by putting God back at the center, and thus—by
putting God back at the center of the life of the Church,
at the center of the life of Christians—Benedict let us
have the ecclesial experience of a life that has God as its
center! "The existence of the Church is vitally dependent
on the correct celebration of the liturgy.... The Church
is in danger when the primacy of God no longer appears
in the liturgy and thus in life. The most profound reason
for the crisis that upset the Church lies in the eclipse of
God's priority in the liturgy."[10]

This primacy of God was again underscored by the person of Joseph Ratzinger. At the altar, clothed in vestments
that at times were splendid, thanks to the good taste of his
master of ceremonies, the pope appeared weak, bent over,
as though humanly powerless. He gave no impression of

[9] Preface to the Russian-language edition of vol. 11, *Theology of the Liturgy*,
of the *Collected Works* of Joseph Ratzinger. Reprinted in Benedict XVI, *What
Is Christianity? The Last Writings*, ed. Elio Guerriero and Georg Gänswein (San
Francisco: Ignatius Press, 2023), 57–58.
[10] Ibid.

crushing power or domination. On the contrary, the celebrant radiated meekness, peace, and a profound interior joy. The sight of this frail little white-haired figure at the base of the columns of the Bernini baldachin reminded us of this very beautiful meditation:

> Jesus is the king ... of those whose hearts are free from the longing for power and material riches, the desire and quest for domination over others. Jesus is the king of those who have that interior freedom that makes one capable of overcoming greed, the selfishness that is in the world, and know that God alone is their wealth. Jesus is the poor king among the poor, meek among those who desire to be meek. In this way he is the king of peace, thanks to the power of God, who is the power of goodness, the power of love.... Evil is conquered by good, by love.[11]

Benedict XVI would be that leader who is powerful through meekness. He let the entire Church have this experience of a God who manifests his omnipotence in weakness. One unforgettable, almost eschatological image of this was the weary, smiling pope in the midst of millions of young people at the World Youth Day in Madrid. His assistants were urging him to take refuge from the storm and the wind that blew tempestuously. He remained there, in the midst of his children, silent and meek. He stood like Mary at the foot of the Cross. Millions were looking right at him, at that white cassock beaten by the wind. His silence, his smile at the heart of the storm radiated peace and meekness.

> [God's] omnipotence is not expressed in violence, it is not expressed in the destruction of every adverse power as

[11] General Audience (October 26, 2011).

we might like; rather it is expressed in love, in mercy, in forgiveness, in accepting our freedom, and in the tireless call for conversion of heart, in an attitude only seemingly weak—God seems weak if we think of Jesus Christ who prays, who lets himself be killed. This apparently weak attitude consists of patience, meekness, and love; it shows that this is the real way to be powerful! This is God's power! And this power will win![12]

How well these words express the mystery of Pope Benedict! An apparent weakness that nevertheless manifests God's power!

Benedict would take this to its logical conclusion. He would set out on a true Way of the Cross. His friends betray him; he forgives them! His collaborators abandon him; he excuses them! Should we speak about weakness in the art of governing? I think that there is, instead, the mystical willingness to give the Church a taste of how divine governance is exercised. Nicolas Diat's book states the truth soberly. Some have rebuked him for it. The display of the despicable acts of the Church's enemies, who are sometimes her children, too, is certainly shocking. The names and the works of these schemers will fall into the dungeons of history. The "victorious weakness" of Benedict will remain and will bear fruit.

Attacked from every side, sullied, slandered, betrayed, Benedict the Great teaches:

Saint John Chrysostom, in one of his homilies, comments: "For so long as we are sheep, we conquer: though ten thousand wolves prowl around, we overcome and prevail. But if we become wolves, we are worsted, for the help of our Shepherd departs from us" (*Homily* 33,

[12] General Audience (January 30, 2013).

1: PG 57, 389). Christians must never yield to the temptation to become wolves among wolves; it is not with might, with force, with violence that Christ's kingdom of peace grows, but with the gift of self, with love carried to the extreme, even toward enemies.[13]

With these words, he announced the kind of death that he would die! He offered himself personally in sacrifice for the Church. He taught us how victory is obtained in the Church. This audience is literally the offertory of the life of Benedict the Meek. From then on, his life became the liturgy of the sacrifice.

Those who want to be disciples of the Lord, his envoys, [must] be prepared for the passion and martyrdom, to lose their own life for him, so that in the world goodness, love, and peace may triumph.... We must be willing to pay in person, to suffer misunderstanding, rejection, persecution in the first person. It is not the sword of the conqueror that builds peace, but the sword of the suffering, of whoever gives up his or her own life.[14]

He would give his life for the Church, Vicar of the Crucified until the end. His resignation had for us the flavor of Good Friday. The sacrifice was consummated. However, Benedict the Mystic did not stop there. He led the Church in a new experience: that of silence and incessant prayer. His retreat to the minuscule monastery in the Vatican Gardens inaugurated a sort of Holy Saturday, a time of silence, prayer, and recollection.

Once again he made everyone understand, this time by his contemplative silence, that God alone matters. His life

---

[13] General Audience (October 26, 2011).
[14] Ibid.

became the manifestation of this primacy of God: "We must relearn the primacy of the interior life and to give it priority over all our activism; the mystical component of Christianity must regain its vigor."[15] His silence in these recent years has been like a challenge to worldly agitation, political calculations, and human pettiness.

In a world that seeks to create for itself a fluid religion to match its lukewarmness, he made us experience the totality of God. God alone suffices!

And here we are, then, on the evening of this Holy Saturday: lost, orphaned disciples. What angel will come to announce to us the Sunday of Easter? Who will give us light? Benedict gives us the answer: "Nothing can put us in contact with the beauty of Christ better than the world of beauty created by faith, and the light on the faces of the saints, through which his own light becomes visible."[16]

In the night of our times, the humble and great face of Benedict XVI will be our light for a long time!

[15] Joseph Ratzinger, "The Church on the Threshold of the Third Millennium" (lecture, Notre-Dame Cathedral, Paris, April 8, 2001).

[16] Joseph Ratzinger, "Wounded by the Arrow of Beauty" (lecture, Rimini, Italy, August 23, 2002).

Part Three

A Spiritual Itinerary
with Benedict XVI

I

The God of Jesus Christ

We take on our lips the words through which we were made Christians, and we consciously accept into our personal life something that was bestowed on us in baptism without any active contribution or reflection on our part. On that occasion, water was poured over us, and the following words were spoken: "I baptize you in the name of the Father and of the Son and of the Holy Spirit." The Church makes a man a Christian by pronouncing the name of the triune God. In this way, she has expressed 'since the very beginning what she considers the most decisive element of the Christian existence, namely, faith in the triune God.

This disappoints us. It is so far removed from our life. It is so useless and so incomprehensible. If some brief formula must be used, then we expect something attractive and exciting, something that immediately strikes us as important for man and for his life. And yet the essential point is precisely what is stated here: the primary concern in Christianity is, not the Church or man, but God. Christianity is not oriented to our own hopes, fears, and needs, but to God, to his sovereignty and power. The first

This text is extracted, with corrections, from Joseph Cardinal Ratzinger, *The God of Jesus Christ: Meditations on the Triune God*, trans. Brian McNeil (San Francisco: Ignatius Press, 2008), 26–29, 51–55.

proposition of the Christian faith and the fundamental orientation of Christian conversion is: "God is."

But what does this mean? What does it mean in our daily life in this world of ours? Let us begin by saying that God exists and, consequently, that the "gods" are not God. Accordingly, we must worship him, no one else. But, one might ask, are not the gods long since dead anyway? Is this not perfectly obvious and, hence, an empty affirmation? But one who looks attentively at reality must counter this response with a question of his own: Has idolatry really ceased in our day? Is there really no longer anything that is worshipped alongside God and against God? Is it not rather the case that, after the "death of God", the gods are ascending once more from the depths with a terrible power?

Martin Luther offered an impressive formulation of this reality in his *Large Catechism*: "What does it mean to have a god, or what is God? *Answer*: A god means that from which we are to expect every good and to which we are to take refuge in every distress, so that to have a god is nothing else than to trust and believe him from the heart; as I have often said that the confidence and faith of the heart alone make both God and an idol."[1] In what then do we place our trust? In what do we believe? Have not money, power, prestige, public opinion, and sex become powers before which men bow down and which they serve like gods? Would not the world look different if these gods were to be deposed from their throne?

God is—and, therefore, that which is true and right is superior to all our goals and interests. That which is worthless in earthly terms has a worth. The adoration of

---

[1] *Triglot Concordia: The Symbolical Books of the Evangelical Lutheran Church*, trans. E. Bente and W. H. Dau (St. Louis, 1921), pp. 565ff. The problematic nature of this text is exposed acutely by P. Hacker, *Das Ich im Glauben bei Martin Luther* (Graz, 1966), pp. 21ff., but we need not discuss this in the present context.

God himself, true adoration, exists, protecting man from the dictatorship of goals. Only this adoration is able to protect him from the dictatorship of idols.

God is—and this also means that all of us are his creatures. Only creatures, indeed; but precisely because we are creatures, we have our true origin in God. We are creatures whom he has willed and whom he has destined for eternity. This is also true of my neighbor, the one beside me whom I may not find at all attractive. Man is not the product of chance. He is not the outcome of a mere struggle for existence that ensures the victory of that which conforms to some goal or other or of that which is able to get its way at the expense of others. No, man owes his origin to God's creative love.

God is—and here we must underline that little word *is*. For God truly is: in other words, he is at work, he acts, and he can act. He is not a remote origin, nor is he some indeterminate "goal of our transcending". He has not abdicated in favor of his world-machine; he has not lost his own function in a world where everything would function autonomously without him. No, the world is and remains *his* world. The present is his time—not the past. He can act, and he does act in a very real way now, in this world and in our life. Do we trust him? When we make plans for our life, for our day-to-day existence, do we see him as a reality? Have we understood the meaning of the first table of the Ten Commandments, which is the truly fundamental challenge to human life, in keeping with the first three requests of the Lord's Prayer, which take up this first table and seek to make it the fundamental orientation of our spirit and our life?

God is—and the Christian faith adds: God is as Father, Son, and Holy Spirit, three and one. This is the very heart of Christianity, but it is so often shrouded in a silence born of perplexity. Has the Church perhaps gone one step too far here? Ought we not rather leave something so great and inaccessible as God in his inaccessibility? Can something like the Trinity have any real meaning for us? Well, it is certainly true that the proposition that "God is three and God is one" is and remains the expression of his otherness, which is infinitely greater than we and transcends all our thinking and our existence. But if this proposition had nothing to say to us, it would not have been revealed. And as a matter of fact, it could be clothed in human language ouly because it had already penetrated human thinking and living to some extent. . . .

The Book of Job and Suffering

This experience [of suffering] shatters the original joy in life (Job 10:18):

> Why did you bring me forth from the womb?
> Would that I had died before any eye had seen me.

Behind Job's cry stand today the millions who perished namelessly in the gas chambers of Auschwitz and in the prisons of dictatorships of the left and the right. The accusers shout ever more loudly: "Where is your God?" No doubt, such words are often an expression of cynicism rather than of genuine respect in the face of the terrible character of human suffering. But the lamentation is true. Where are you, God? Who are you, that you keep silent?

Only God himself can reply. He has not done so in a conclusive manner. He has not done it in such a way that one could lay the answer on one's desk and check the calculations. But nor has he been completely silent.

It is true that his final word has not yet been spoken; in the Resurrection of Jesus, it has only begun. And this is always a word that demands not only man's understanding, but also his heart. This is how it begins with Job: God intervenes in the debate, and he does not take the side of those who are defending him. He rejects as a blasphemy the apologia that makes him the cruel executioner of the pettyminded calculations of a *quid pro quo* righteousness. It is not the cries of Job that have offended God, but rather the precision of those who dare to present a terrible retributive mechanism as the face of God. And yet, nothing is explained to Job. He is only made aware of his littleness, of the poverty of the perspective from which he looks at the world. He learns to be still, to be silent, to hope. His heart is widened—and that is all. This humble act of falling silent as the first step of wisdom should concern us, too. It is a striking fact that the accusation against God hardly ever comes from the lips of those who suffer in this world. It is almost always pronounced by the well-fed onlookers, who themselves have never suffered. In this world, the hymn of God's praise ascends from the furnaces of those who suffer: the story of the three young men in the fiery furnace contains a deeper truth than all the learned treatises.[2]

The reply to Job is only a beginning, a groping anticipation of the answer that God gives with the action of his own Son in the Cross and Resurrection of Jesus Christ. Here too, there is nothing that can be added and checked. God's answer is not an explanation but an action. The answer is a sharing in suffering—not as a mere feeling, but as reality. God's compassion has flesh. It means scourging, crowning with thorns, crucifixion, a tomb. He has entered

[2] I repeat here in part what I have already argued in *Dogma und Verkündigung* [*Dogma and Preaching*], pp. 331–39.

into our suffering. What does this mean, what can it mean? We can learn this before the great images of the crucified Jesus and the *Pietà*, where the Mother holds her dead Son. Before such images and in them, men have perceived a transformation of suffering: they have experienced that God himself dwells in the innermost sphere of their sufferings and that they became one with him precisely in their bruises. We are not speaking here of some cheap "consolation", for this experience created that love for sufferers that we see exemplified in Francis of Assisi or Elizabeth of Hungary. The crucified Christ has not removed suffering from the world. But through his Cross, he has changed men, opening their hearts to their suffering sisters and brothers and thereby strengthening and purifying them all. From him arises that "reverence for what is in our midst" that is lacking in pagan humanity and that expires where faith in the Crucified One ceases to exist. Are we not gradually beginning to grasp—thanks to all the problems connected with our "health service"—that there are some things that money cannot buy? And is not the change in contemporary society letting us gradually see something of that change that was once brought about by faith and was much more than an empty "consolation"?

We must take one further step. The Cross was not God's last word in Jesus Christ. The tomb did not hold him fast: he is risen, and God speaks to us through the Risen One. The rich glutton in hell asked that Lazarus might appear to his brothers and warn them lest they share his dreadful fate. He thinks: "If someone goes to them from the dead, they will repent" (Lk 16:27ff.). But the true Lazarus *has* come. He is here, and he speaks to us: This life is not everything. There is an eternity. Today, it is very unmodern to say this, even in theology. To speak of life beyond death looks like a flight from life here on earth. But what if it is true?

Can one simply pass it by? Can one dismiss it as mere consolation? Is it not precisely this reality that bestows on life its seriousness, its freedom, its hope?

Man is the image of God, but this image looks at us only in multiple distortions. This affirmation, in the pure sense, is true only of Jesus Christ, who is the restored image of God. But what God do we see in him? A misunderstood theology has left many people with a completely false image, the image of a cruel God who demands the blood of his own Son. They have read out of the Cross the image of Job's friends and have turned their backs on this God in horror. But the opposite is true! The biblical God demands no human sacrifices. When he appears in the course of the history of religion, human sacrifice ceases. Before Abraham can slaughter Isaac, God speaks and stops him; the ram takes the place of the child. The cult of Yahweh begins when the sacrifice of the firstborn, which was demanded by the ancestral religion of Abraham, is replaced by his obedience and his faith—the external substitute, the ram, is only the expression of this deeper reality, which is not a replacement, but rather looks ahead to the future fulfillment.[3] For the God of Israel, human sacrifice is an abomination; Moloch, the god of human sacrifices, is the embodiment of the false god who is opposed by faith in Yahweh.[4] For the God of Israel, it is not the death of a man but his life that is the act of worship. Irenaeus of Lyons expressed this in the wonderful formula: "Gloria Dei homo vivens" (The living man is the glory of

[3] These brief words do not exhaust the theological depths of the sacrifice of Isaac and of its orientation to Christ. For a further elaboration, cf. L. Massignon, "Die drei Gebete Abrahams", *Internationale katholische Zeitschrift Communio* 4 (1975): 19–28.

[4] Cf. W. Kornfeld, "Moloch", in *Bibellexikon*, ed. H. Haag, 2nd ed., pp. 1163f., with bibliography (Einsiedeln, 1968).

God). And this is the kind of "human sacrifice", of worship, that God demands." But in that case, what does the Lord's Cross mean? It is the form of that love which has totally accepted man and has therefore descended even into his guilt and his death. In this way, the love became a "sacrifice": as the love unbounded that takes man, the lost sheep, on its shoulders and bears him back to the Father through the night of his sin. Since then, a new form of suffering has existed: suffering not as curse but as a love that transforms the world.

II

Encountering Christ

Homily at the Funeral Mass of Monsignor Luigi Giussani, Milan, February 24, 2005

Dear brother bishops and brother priests,

"The disciples were glad when they saw the Lord" (Jn 20:20). These words from today's Gospel show us the center of the personality and life of our dear Father Giussani.

Father Giussani grew up in a house that was—to use his words—poor in bread but rich in music, so that from the very beginning he was touched, or, better, wounded, by the desire for beauty. He was not satisfied, however, with just any ordinary beauty, with beauty in a banal sense; he sought, rather, Beauty itself, infinite Beauty, and thus he found Christ. In Christ he found true beauty, the path of life, true joy.

When he was only a boy, together with other youths, he started a community by the name of Studium Christi. Their plan was to speak of nothing but Christ, because everything else seemed to be a waste of time. Later, of course, he was to overcome this one-sidedness, but the

Joseph Cardinal Ratzinger, "Funeral Homily for Msgr. Luigi Giussani", *Communio: International Theological Review* 31, no. 4 (2004): 685–87. Translation modified for style by Ignatius Press.

substance for him would always remain the same: only Christ gives meaning to the rest of our life. Father Giussani kept the gaze of his life, of his heart, always fixed on Christ. It was in this way that he understood that Christianity is not an intellectual system, a collection of dogmas, or moralism. Christianity is instead an encounter, a love story; it is an event.

This love affair with Christ, this love story that was the whole of Giussani's life, was at the same time quite far removed from any superficial enthusiasm or vague romanticism. Seeing Christ, Giussani truly knew that to encounter Christ means to follow him. This encounter is a road, a journey, a journey that also passes—as we heard in the psalm—through the "valley of the shadow of death" (Ps 23:4). In the Gospel we heard of the final darkness of Christ's suffering, of the seeming absence of God, of the eclipse of the Sun of the world. Giussani knew that to follow means to pass through a "valley of the shadow of death", to take the way of the Cross, and all the while to live in true joy.

Why is this so? The Lord himself translated the mystery of the Cross, which is really the mystery of love, by means of a formula that expresses the reality of our life in its entirety. The Lord says, "Whoever seeks to gain his life will lose it, but whoever loses his life will preserve it" (Lk 17:33).

Father Giussani truly desired not to have life for his own sake: instead, he gave life, and it is precisely in this that he found it not only for himself, but for so many others. He lived out what we heard in the Gospel. He wished not to be served but to serve. He was a faithful servant of the Gospel. He gave away all the wealth of his heart. He gave away all the divine wealth of the Gospel that permeated him. By this service, by this giving of his life, this life of his has borne rich fruit, as we can see in this very moment. He has truly become the father of many, and by guiding people not to himself but to Christ, he has truly conquered hearts. He has helped to make the world better; he has helped to open up the doors of the world to Heaven.

The centrality of Christ in his life also brought about in Father Giussani the gift of discernment, of deciphering correctly the signs of the times during an age that is, as we know, very difficult and filled with temptations and errors. Consider 1968 and the following years, when a first group of his followers went to Brazil and found itself face to face with extreme poverty and misery. What could be done? How to respond? And the temptation was great to say, "Just for the moment we will have to set Christ aside, set God aside, because there are more pressing needs. First we have to change structures, fix the external things; first we must improve the earth, and after that we will be able to find Heaven again." The great temptation of the moment was to transform Christianity into moralism and moralism into politics, that is, to substitute doing for believing. Because what does it mean to believe? Someone may say: "We have to do something right now." By substituting moralism for faith, doing for believing, though, we retreat into particularism. Above all, we lose the criteria for judging and the guideposts that orient us in the right direction. The final result, instead of constructive growth, is division.

Monsignor Giussani, with his fearless and unfailing faith, knew that even in this situation it is Christ, the encounter with Christ, that remains central. Whoever does not give God gives too little; and whoever does not give God, whoever does not enable people to see God in the face of Christ, does not build anything up but, rather, wastes human activity in false, ideological dogmatism, and so ultimately only destroys.

Don Giussani preserved the centrality of Christ and it was exactly in this way that he was able, by means of social works and needed services, to help mankind in this difficult world, where Christians bear an enormous and urgent responsibility for the poor.

The believer, too, must pass through the "valley of the shadow of death", the dark valley of discernment, and so also of adversity, opposition, and ideological hostility. He must face even threats to physically eliminate him and those he loves, in order to rid the world of this voice that refuses to rest content merely with action, but bears a greater message and thus also a greater light.

In the strength of faith, Monsignor Giussani passed undaunted through these dark valleys and, given the freshness he brought, also encountered difficulties fitting in within the Church. It is always the case that if the Holy Spirit, in accord with the needs of the times, creates something new—which is in reality a return to the origins—it is difficult to find the right direction and to attain the peaceful unity of the great communion of the universal Church. Father Giussani's love for Christ was also love for the Church, and thus he always remained a faithful servant, faithful to the Holy Father and faithful to his bishops.

Through his foundations, he also interpreted the mystery of the Church in a new way.

"Communion and Liberation" immediately brings to mind the modern era's particular discovery, freedom, while also recalling Saint Ambrose's phrase "Ubi fides est libertas" [Where there is faith, there is freedom]. Cardinal Biffi drew our attention to the close accord between this phrase of Saint Ambrose and the foundation of Communion and Liberation. Focusing on freedom as a gift proper to faith, he also told us that if it is to be a true human freedom, that is, freedom in truth, then freedom needs communion. An isolated freedom, a freedom solely for the sake of the "I", would be a lie, and would necessarily destroy human communion. To be true, and, therefore, efficacious, freedom needs communion, and not just any communion but ultimately communion with truth itself, with love itself, with Christ, with the trinitarian God. This is the path to communion that creates freedom and brings joy.

The other foundation, Memores Domini, brings to mind once more the second Gospel from today: the memory that the Lord gave us in the Holy Eucharist, a memory that is not merely the remembrance of the past, but a memory that creates in the present, a memory in which he gives himself over into our hands and into our hearts, and thereby makes us live.

Through valleys of darkness: in the last period of his life, Father Giussani had to pass through the dark valley of sickness, of infirmity, of pain, of suffering, but here, too, his eyes were fixed on Jesus and so he remained true in the midst of all the suffering. Seeing Jesus, he was able to rejoice; he knew the presence of the joy of the Risen One, who even in the Passion is the Risen One and gives us true light and joy. He knew, too, that, as the psalm says, even passing through this valley, "I fear no evil; for you are with me ... and I shall dwell in the house of the LORD for ever" (Ps 23:4–6). This was his great strength: to know that "You are with me."

My dear faithful, above all my dear young people, let us take this message to heart. Let us not lose sight of Christ. Let us not forget that without God nothing good can be built up, and that God remains an enigma to us when he is not recognized in the face of Christ.

Now your dear friend Father Giussani has reached the other world. We are convinced that the doors of the

Father's house have opened. We are sure that now these words have fully come to pass: "The disciples were glad when they saw the Lord." He is rejoicing with a joy that no one can take from him. In this moment we wish to thank the Lord for the great gift of this priest, this faithful servant of the Gospel, this father. We entrust his soul, and ours, to the goodness of his Lord.

III

A Heart Pierced by Beauty

Speech at the Communion and Liberation Meeting in Rimini, August 24, 2002

Every year, in the Liturgy of the Hours for the season of Lent, I am struck anew by a paradox in Vespers for Monday of the second week of the Psalter. Here, side by side, are two antiphons, one for the season of Lent, the other for Holy Week. Both introduce Psalm 45, but they present strikingly contradictory interpretations. The psalm describes the wedding of the king, his beauty, his virtues, his mission, and then becomes an exaltation of his bride. In the season of Lent, Psalm 45 is framed by the same antiphon used for the rest of the year. The second verse of the psalm says: "You are the fairest of the sons of men; grace is poured upon your lips".

Naturally, the Church reads this psalm as a poetic-prophetic representation of Christ's spousal relationship with his Church. She recognizes Christ as the fairest of men, and the grace poured upon his lips points to the inner beauty of his words, the glory of his proclamation.

Joseph Cardinal Ratzinger, Message at the Communion and Liberation Meeting (Rimini, Italy, August 24, 2002), https://www.vatican.va/roman _curia/congregations/cfaith/documents/rc_con_cfaith_doc_20020824 _ratzinger-cl-rimini_en.html. Translation modified for style by Ignatius Press.

So it is not merely the external beauty of the Redeemer's appearance that is glorified: rather, the beauty of Truth appears in him, the beauty of God himself, who draws us to himself and, at the same time, captures us with the wound of Love, the holy passion (*eros*), that enables us to go forth together, with and in the Church his Bride, to meet the Love who calls us.

On Monday of Holy Week, however, the Church changes the antiphon and invites us to interpret the Psalm in the light of Isaiah 53:2: "He had no form or comeliness that we should look at him, and no beauty that we should desire him." How can we reconcile this? The appearance of the "fairest of the sons of men" is so wretched that no one desires to look at him. Pilate presented him to the crowd, saying, "Here is the man!" (Jn 19:5) to rouse sympathy for the crushed and battered man, in whom no external beauty remained.

Augustine, who in his youth wrote a book on the beautiful and the harmonious [*De pulchro et apto*] and who appreciated beauty in words, in music, and in the figurative arts, had a keen appreciation of this paradox and realized that in this regard, the great Greek philosophy of the beautiful was not to be simply rejected but rather, to be dramatically called into question; and what the beautiful might be, what beauty might mean, would have to be debated and experienced anew. Referring to the paradox contained in these texts, he spoke of the contrasting blasts of "two trumpets" produced by the same breath, the same Spirit. He knew that a paradox is contrast and not contradiction. Both quotations come from the same Spirit who inspires all Scripture, but sounds different notes in it. It is in this way that he sets us before the totality of true Beauty, of Truth itself.

In the first place, the text of Isaiah supplies the question that interested the Fathers of the Church: whether or not

Christ was beautiful. Implicit here is the more radical question of whether beauty is true, or whether it is ugliness that leads us to the deepest truth of reality. Whoever believes in God, in the God who manifested himself precisely in the altered appearance of Christ crucified as love "to the end" (Jn 13:1), knows that beauty is truth and truth beauty; but in the suffering Christ, he learns that the beauty of truth also embraces offense, pain, and even the dark mystery of death, and that this beauty can only be found in accepting suffering, not in ignoring it.

Certainly, the consciousness that beauty has something to do with pain was also present in the Greek world. Let us take Plato's *Phaedrus* as an example. Plato contemplates the encounter with beauty as the salutary emotional shock that makes man leave his shell and sparks his "enthusiasm" by attracting him to what is other than himself. Man, says Plato, has lost the original perfection that was conceived for him. He is now perennially searching for the healing primitive form. Nostalgia and longing impel him to pursue the quest; beauty prevents him from being content with just daily life. It causes him to suffer. In a Platonic sense, we could say that the arrow of nostalgia pierces man and wounds him, and in this way gives him wings, lifts him upward toward the transcendent. In his discourse in the *Symposium*, Aristophanes says that lovers do not know what they really want from each other. From the search for what is more than their pleasure, it is obvious that the souls of both are thirsting for something other than amorous gratification. But the heart cannot express this "other" thing: "it has only a vague perception of what it truly wants and wonders about it as an enigma".

In the fourteenth century, in the book *The Life in Christ* by the Byzantine theologian Nicholas Cabasilas, we rediscover Plato's experience in which the ultimate object of nostalgia, transformed by the new Christian experience, continues to be nameless. Cabasilas says: "When men have a longing so great that it surpasses human nature and eagerly desire and are able to accomplish things beyond human thought, it is the Bridegroom who has smitten them with this longing. It is He who has sent a ray of His beauty into their eyes. The greatness of the wound shows the dart which has struck home, the longing indicates who has inflicted the wound."[1]

The beautiful wounds, but this is exactly how it summons man to his final destiny. What Plato said, and, more than 1,500 years later, Cabasilas, has nothing to do with superficial aestheticism and irrationalism or with the flight from clarity and the importance of reason. The beautiful is knowledge, certainly, but in a superior form, since it arouses man to the real greatness of the truth. Here Cabasilas has remained entirely Greek, since he puts knowledge first when he says, "In fact it is knowing that causes love and gives birth to it.... Since this knowledge is sometimes very ample and complete and at other times imperfect, it follows that the [love potion] has a corresponding effect."[2]

He is not content to leave this assertion in general terms. In his characteristically rigorous thought, he distinguishes between two kinds of knowledge. The first is knowledge through instruction, which remains, so to speak, "secondhand" and does not imply any direct contact with reality itself. The second type of knowledge, on the other hand, is knowledge through personal experience, through a direct relationship with the reality. "Therefore we do not love it to the extent that it is a worthy object of love, and

[1] Nicholas Cabasilas, *The Life in Christ*, trans. Carmino J. deCatanzaro (Crestwood, N.Y.: St. Vladimir's Seminary Press, 1998), 90.
[2] Ibid., 89.

since we have not perceived the very form itself we do not experience its proper effect."[3]

True knowledge is being struck by the arrow of Beauty that wounds man, moved by reality; "now it is Christ Himself who is present and in an ineffable manner disposes and forms the souls of men."[4]

Being struck and overcome by the beauty of Christ is a more real, more profound knowledge than mere rational deduction. Of course we must not underrate the importance of theological reflection, of exact and precise theological thought; it remains absolutely necessary. But to move from here to disdain or reject the impact produced by the response of the heart in the encounter with beauty as a true form of knowledge would impoverish us and dry up our faith and our theology. We must rediscover this form of knowledge; it is a pressing need of our time.

Starting with this concept, Hans Urs von Balthasar built his magnum opus of theological aesthetics. Many of its details have passed into theological work, while his fundamental approach, in truth the essential element of the whole work, has not been so readily accepted. Of course, this is not just, or principally, a theological problem, but a problem of pastoral life, which has to foster the human person's encounter with the beauty of faith. All too often arguments fall on deaf ears because in our world too many contradictory arguments compete with one another, so much so that we are spontaneously reminded of the medieval theologians' description of reason, that it "has a wax nose": in other words, it can be pointed in any direction, if one is clever enough. Everything makes sense, is so convincing; whom should we trust?

[3] Ibid., 90.
[4] Ibid., 91.

The encounter with the beautiful can become the wound of the arrow that strikes the heart and in this way opens our eyes, so that later we take the criteria for judgment from this experience and can correctly evaluate the arguments. For me an unforgettable experience was the Bach concert that Leonard Bernstein conducted in Munich after the sudden death of Karl Richter. I was sitting next to the Lutheran bishop [Johannes] Hanselmann. When the last note of one of the great Thomaskantor cantatas triumphantly faded away, we looked at each other spontaneously and right then we said: "Anyone who has heard this knows that the faith is true." The music had such an extraordinary force of reality that we realized, no longer by deduction, but by the impact on our hearts, that it could not have originated from nothingness, but could only have come to be through the power of the Truth that became real in the composer's inspiration. Isn't the same thing evident when we allow ourselves to be moved by the icon of the Trinity of Rublev? In the art of the icons, as in the great Western paintings of the Romanesque and Gothic periods, the experience described by Cabasilas, starting with interiority, is visibly portrayed and can be shared.

In a rich way, Pavel Evdokimov has brought to light the interior pathway that an icon establishes. An icon does not simply reproduce what can be perceived by the senses, but rather it presupposes, as he says, "a fasting of sight". Inner perception must free itself from the impression of the merely sensible, and in prayer and ascetical effort acquire a new and deeper capacity to see, to perform the passage from what is merely external to the profundity of reality, in such a way that the artist can see what the senses as such do not see, and what actually appears in what can be perceived: the splendor of the glory of God, the "glory of God in the face of Christ" (2 Cor 1:6).

To admire the icons, and the great masterpieces of Christian art in general, leads us on an inner way, a way of overcoming ourselves; thus, in this purification of vision that is a purification of the heart, it reveals the beautiful to us, or at least a ray of it. In this way we are brought into contact with the power of the truth. I have often affirmed my conviction that the true apology of Christian faith, the most convincing demonstration of its truth against every denial, are the saints and the beauty that the faith has generated. Today, for faith to grow, we must lead ourselves and the people we meet to encounter the saints and to enter into contact with the Beautiful.

Now, however, we still have to respond to an objection. We have already rejected the assumption that claims that what has just been said is a flight into the irrational, into mere aestheticism.

Rather, it is the opposite that is true: this is the very way in which reason is freed from dullness and made ready to act.

Today another objection has even greater weight: the message of beauty is thrown into complete doubt by the power of falsehood, seduction, violence, and evil. Can the beautiful be genuine, or, in the end, is it only an illusion? Isn't reality perhaps basically evil? The fear that in the end it is not the arrow of the beautiful that leads us to the truth, but that falsehood, all that is ugly and vulgar, may constitute the true "reality" has at all times caused people anguish. At present this has been expressed in the assertion that after Auschwitz it was no longer possible to write poetry; after Auschwitz it was no longer possible to speak of a God who is good. People wondered: Where was God when the gas chambers were operating? This objection, which seemed reasonable enough before Auschwitz as well when one realized all the atrocities of history, shows that in any case a purely harmonious concept of beauty is not enough. It cannot stand up to the confrontation with the gravity of the questioning about God, truth, and beauty. Apollo, who for Plato's Socrates was "the God" and the guarantor of unruffled beauty as "the truly divine" is absolutely no longer sufficient.

In this way, we return to the "two trumpets" of the Bible with which we started, to the paradox of being able to say of Christ: "You are the fairest of the sons of men" and "He had no form or comeliness that we should look at him, and no beauty that we should desire him." In the Passion of Christ, the Greek aesthetic—which deserves admiration for its perceived contact with the Divine, but which nevertheless remained incapable of expressing it—is not removed but transcended. The experience of the beautiful has received new depth and new realism. The One who is Beauty itself let himself be slapped in the face, spat upon, crowned with thorns; the Shroud of Turin can help us imagine this in a realistic way. However, in his face that is so disfigured, there appears genuine, extreme beauty: the beauty of love that goes "to the end"; for this reason it is revealed as greater than falsehood and violence. Whoever has perceived this beauty knows that truth, and not falsehood, is the real aspiration of the world. It is not falsity that is "true", but indeed, the Truth. It is, as it were, a new trick of what is false to present itself as "truth" and to say to us: Over and above me there is basically nothing. Stop seeking or even loving the truth; in doing so you are on the wrong track. The icon of the crucified Christ sets us free from this deception that is so widespread today. However, it imposes a condition: that we let ourselves be wounded by him, and that we believe in the Love who can risk setting aside his external beauty to proclaim, in this way, the truth of the beautiful.

Falsehood, however, has another stratagem. [It offers] a beauty that is deceptive and false, a blinding beauty that does not bring human beings out of themselves to open them to the ecstasy of rising to the heights, but rather locks them entirely in themselves. Such beauty does not reawaken a longing for the ineffable, readiness for sacrifice, or the abandonment of self, but instead stirs up desire, the will for power, possession, and pleasure. It is that type of experience of beauty of which Genesis speaks in the account of the first human sin. Eve saw that the fruit of the tree was "beautiful" to eat and was "a delight to the eyes" (Gen 3:6). The beautiful, as she experienced it, aroused in her a desire for possession, making her, as it were, turn in upon herself. Who would not recognize, for example, in advertising, the images made with supreme skill that are created to tempt the human being irresistibly, to make him want to grab everything and seek passing satisfaction rather than being open to the other?

So it is that Christian art today is caught between two fires (as perhaps it has always been): It must oppose the cult of the ugly, which says that everything beautiful is a deception, and only the representation of what is crude, low, and vulgar is the truth, the true illumination of knowledge. And it must counter the deceptive beauty that diminishes the human being instead of making him great, and for this reason is false.

Is there anyone who does not know Dostoyevsky's often quoted sentence "The Beautiful will save us"? However, people usually forget that Dostoyevsky is referring here to the redeeming beauty of Christ. We must learn to see him. If we not only know him in words but are struck by the arrow of his paradoxical beauty, then we will know him truly, and know him not simply because we have heard others speak about him. Then we will have found the beauty of Truth, of the Truth that redeems. Nothing can bring us into closer contact with the beauty of Christ himself than the world of beauty created by faith and the light that shines in the faces of the saints, through which his own light becomes visible.

IV

The Church on the Threshold
of the Third Millennium

Lenten Address at Notre-Dame Cathedral
in Paris, April 8, 2001

Your Eminence, dear brothers and sisters,

I recently read in a newspaper about a German intellectual who said of himself that where the question of God was concerned, he was an agnostic: it was just not possible, he said, either to demonstrate the existence of God or absolutely to exclude it, so the matter would remain undecided. He said he was utterly convinced, on the other hand, of the existence of hell; a glance at the television was enough for him to see that it existed. While the first half of this confession corresponds entirely with modern consciousness, the second appears strange, indeed, incomprehensible—at least when you first hear it. For how can you believe in hell if there is no God? When you look closer at it, this statement turns out to be entirely logical: hell is,

This English translation is taken, with corrections, from Joseph Cardinal Ratzinger, *Pilgrim Fellowship of Faith: The Church as Communion*, ed. Stephan Otto Horn and Vinzenz Pfnür, trans. Henry Taylor (San Francisco: Ignatius Press, 2005), 284–98.

precisely, the situation in which God is absent. That is the definition of it: where God is not there, where no glimmer of his presence can any longer penetrate, that place is hell. Perhaps our daily look at the television does not show us that, but certainly a look at the history of the twentieth century does, for it has left us places like Auschwitz and the Gulag Archipelago and names like Hitler, Stalin, and Pol Pot. Anyone who reads the witnesses' accounts of those anti-worlds will encounter visions that for atrocities and destruction rival Dante's descent into hell, are indeed even more frightful, because there appear dimensions of evil that Dante could have had no way of perceiving in advance. These hells were constructed in order to be able to bring about the future world of the man who was his own master, who was no longer supposed to need any God. Man was offered in sacrifice to the Moloch of that utopia of a God-free world, a world set free from God, for man was now wholly in control of his destiny and knew no limits to his ability to determine things, because there was no longer any God set over him, because no light of the image of God shone forth anymore from man.

Wherever God is not, hell comes into existence: it consists simply in his absence. That may also come about in subtle forms and almost always does so under cover of the idea of something beneficial for people. If nowadays there is a traffic in human organs, if fetuses are being formed to provide a supply of such organs or in order to further research into health and sickness, it is for many the humanitarian content of these actions that is apparent; yet with the contempt for human beings that is inherent in them, with this way of using people, and even using them up, we are in fact, after all, again on our way down to hell. That does not imply that there cannot be—as in fact there are— atheists with high ethics. Yet I venture to maintain that these ethics are based on the lingering glimmer of the light that once came from Sinai—the light of God. Far-distant stars, now already dead, may still be shining upon us. Even when God seems to be dead, his light may still be around. Yet Nietzsche rightly pointed out that the moment when the news that God is dead has reached everywhere, the moment in which his light would finally be extinguished, can only be frightful.

Why am I saying all this in a meditation on the question of what we Christians have to do today, in this historic moment of ours at the beginning of the third millennium? I am saying it because it is on that very basis that our task as Christians becomes clear. It is both simple and very great: it is a matter of witnessing to God, of opening up the barred and darkened windows so that his light may shine among us, that there may be room for his presence. For it is true, conversely, that where God is, there is Heaven: there, even in the tribulations of our daily living, life becomes bright. Christianity is not a complicated philosophy that has in the meanwhile also become obsolete, not a package of dogmas and rules beyond being grasped as a whole. Christian faith is being touched by God and witnessing to him. That is why Paul, on the Areopagus, described his task and his intention as wishing to make known to the Athenians, whom he addressed as representative of the peoples of the world, the unknown God—the God who had emerged from his hiddenness, who had made himself known, and who could therefore be proclaimed by him (Acts 17:16–34). The reference to the expression "the unknown god" presupposes that man, in not knowing, still does know about God in some way; it responds to the situation of the agnostic, who does not know God personally and yet cannot exclude him. It presupposes that man is in some sense waiting for God and yet cannot of his own resources reach him, so that he is in need of preaching, of the hand that helps him over into the sphere of his presence.

Thus we can say: the Church is there so that God, the living God, may be made known—so that man may learn to live with God, live in his sight and in fellowship with him. The Church is there to prevent the advance of hell upon earth and to make the earth fit to live in through the light of God. On the basis of God's presence, and only through him, is it humanized. We may also formulate this from the third petition of the Our Father: "Thy will be done on earth, as it is in heaven." Wherever God's will is carried out is Heaven, and there earth can become Heaven. That is why it is a matter of making it possible to discern God's will and of bringing man's will into harmony with God's will. For one cannot know God in a merely academic way; one cannot merely take note of his existence, as for instance I may note the existence of distant stars or that of the data of past history. Knowledge of God may be compared to the knowledge of someone in love: it concerns me as a whole; it also demands my will; and it comes to nothing if it does not attain this all-embracing assent.

But in saying this I have gotten ahead of myself. For the moment, let us note that for the Church, it is never merely a matter of maintaining her membership or even of increasing or broadening her own membership. The Church is not there for her own sake. She cannot be like an association that, in difficult circumstances, is simply trying to keep its head above water. She has a task to perform for the world, for mankind. The only reason she has to survive is because her disappearance would drag humanity into the whirlpool of the eclipse of God and, thus, into the eclipse, indeed, the destruction, of all that is human. We are not fighting for our own survival; we know that we have been entrusted

with a mission that lays upon us a responsibility for everyone. That is why the Church has to measure herself, and be
measured by others, by the extent to which the presence
of God, the knowledge of him, and the acceptance of his
will are alive within her. A church that was merely an organization pursuing its own ends would be the caricature of
a church. To the extent to which she is revolving around
herself and looks only to the aims necessary for maintaining
herself, she is rendering herself redundant and is in decline,
even if she disposes of considerable means and skillful man-
agement. She can live and be fruitful only if the primacy of
God is alive within her.

The Church is there, not for her own sake, but for mankind. She is there so that the world may become a sphere
for God's presence, the sphere of the covenant between
God and men. Thus, that is what the creation story is saying (Gen 1:1—2:4): the way that the text moves toward the
Sabbath is trying to make clear that creation has an inner
basis and purpose. It is there in order that the covenant
may come to be in which God freely gives his love and
receives the response of love. The idea that the Church is
there for mankind has recently been appearing in a variant
that makes sense to us but jeopardizes the essence of the
matter. People are saying that in recent times the history
of theology and of the Church's understanding of herself
has passed through three stages: from ecclesially centered
to Christ-centered and, finally, God-centered. This, it is
said, represents progress, but it has not yet reached its final
stage. It is clear, people say, that ecclesially centered theology was wrong: the Church should not make herself
the center of things; she is not there for her own sake.
Therefore we moved on to Christ-centered thinking;
Christ was supposed to be at the heart. Then, however, it
was recognized—they say—that Christ, too, points above

and beyond himself to the Father, and thus we arrived at theocentric, God-centered thinking, and this signified at the same time an opening up of the Church to the outside, to other religions: the Church divides people, but Christ also divides, so people say. And then people add: God, too, divides people, since people's images of God contradict one another, and there are religions without a personal God and ways of understanding the world without God. Thus, as a fourth stage, the centrality of the kingdom is postulated, and though this is apparently a development from the Gospel, people call it, no longer the Kingdom of God, but just simply "the kingdom", as a cipher for the better world that is to be built up.

The centrality of the kingdom is supposed to mean that everyone, reaching beyond the boundaries of religions and ideologies, can now work together for the values of the kingdom, which are, to wit, peace, justice, and the conservation of creation. This trio of values has nowadays emerged as a substitute for the lost concept of God and, at the same time, as the unifying formula that could be the basis, beyond all distinctions and differences, for the worldwide community of men of goodwill (and who is not one of them?) and thus might really be able to lead to that better world. That sounds tempting. Who is there who does not feel bound to support the great aim of peace on earth? Who would not be bound to strive for justice to be done, so that finally the glaring differences between classes and races and continents might disappear? And who would not see the need today to defend creation against the modern forms of destruction it suffers? Has God become superfluous, then? Can this trio of values take his place? Yet, how do we know what will bring peace? Where do we find a standard for justice and a way of distinguishing paths that lead there from paths that turn aside? And how are we to know when technology is appropriate to the claims of creation and when it is becoming destructive? Anyone who sees how this trio of values is handled, worldwide, cannot hide the fact that it is increasingly becoming a hotbed of ideologies and that without an all-embracing standard of what is consistent with existence, what is appropriate to creation, and what is humane, it cannot survive intact. Values cannot replace truth; they cannot replace God, for they are only a reflection of him, and without his light their outline becomes blurred.

Thus, we are left with this: without God, the world cannot be bright, and the Church is serving the world by virtue of God living within her and her being transparent for him and carrying him to mankind. And thereby we come at last to the quite practical question: How does that happen? How can we ourselves recognize God, and how can we bring him to other people? I think that for this purpose, several different ways must be interwoven. First there is the way that Paul adopted on the Areopagus— the reference to the capacity to know God that is buried within men, appealing to reason. "[God] is not far from each one of us", Paul says there. "In him we live and move and have our being" (Acts 17:27–28). In the Letter to the Romans, we meet the same idea, still more strongly expressed: "Ever since the creation of the world [God's] invisible nature, namely, his eternal power and deity, has been clearly perceived in the things that have been made" (1:20). Christian faith appeals to reason, to the transparency of creation in revealing the Creator. The Christian religion is a religion of the Logos: "In the beginning was the Word" is how we translate the first sentence of the Gospel of John, which is consciously referring, for its part, to the first sentence of the Bible as such, the account of the creation being carried out through the Word. Yet "word" (*logos*), in the biblical sense, also means reason, with its creative power.

Meanwhile, however, is that sentence about the beginning of the world in the Word, thus understood, still acceptable today? Can the Church still join the Bible today in appealing to reason, in referring to the way creation transparently reveals the creative spirit? There is today a materialistic version of the theory of evolution that presents itself as being the last word in science and lays claim to having made the creative spirit superfluous through its hypotheses, indeed, to have excluded it definitively. Jacques Monod, who elaborated this theory with admirable logical consistency, has commented on his own theory with typical honesty: "The miracle has indeed been 'explained', and yet it remains for us a miracle." And then he quotes the comment that François Mauriac delivered about his theories: "What this professor says is much more incredible yet than what we poor Christians believe." And he responds, "That is just as true as the fact that we cannot succeed in forming a satisfying mental picture of certain abstractions of modern physics. Yet at the same time, we know that such difficulties cannot stand as an argument against a theory that has in its favor the certainties of experience and logic."[1] At that point one must inquire: Which logic? I cannot—and do not want to—take up this dispute here, but I will say only that faith has no reason to quit the field here. The option of thinking that the world originates from reason, and not from unreason, can be rationally maintained even today, though it must of course be formulated in conversation with the genuine findings of natural science. That is one task the Church has today: to

[1] Jacques Monod, *Chance and Necessity* (Harmondsworth: Penguin, 1997) (quotations from pages 171–72 of the German edition).

revive the argument about the rationality of belief or unbe-
lief. Belief is not an opponent of reason, but the advocate
of its true stature, as Pope John Paul II has depicted with
passionate commitment in his encyclical *Faith and Reason*.
The struggle for the new presence of the rationality of
faith is what I regard as an urgent task for the Church in
our century. Faith should not withdraw into its own shell,
behind a decision for which it gives no further reason;
it should not shrink into being no more than a kind of
system of symbols, in which people can make themselves
at home but which would ultimately remain a random
choice among other visions of life and the world. It needs
the wide realm of open reason; it needs the confession
of faith in the Creator God, for without this confession of
faith, even Christology is diminished; it then talks only
indirectly about God, by referring to a particular religious
experience, while this, however, is necessarily limited and
would then become just one experience among others.

The appeal to reason is a great task for the Church, especially today, for whenever faith and reason part company,
both become diseased. Reason becomes cold and loses its
standards of judgment; it becomes cruel, because nothing
is superior to it anymore. The limited understanding of
man is now making decisions alone about what should
happen to creation in the future, about who is allowed to
live and who is being shut out from the banquet of life: the
path to hell, as we have seen, then lies open. Yet faith, too,
becomes diseased without the wide realm of reason. What
dreadful destruction can then come forth from a sick reli-
giosity we can see in abundance in our own present-day
society. It is not without reason that the Book of Revelation portrays sick religion, which has taken leave of the
dimension of belief about creation, as the genuine power
of the Antichrist.

It remains true, of course, that the revelation in creation to which Paul refers in the Areopagus speech and in the Letter to the Romans is not in itself sufficient really to bring man into relationship with God. God has come to meet man. He has shown him his face, opened up his heart to him. "No one has ever seen God; the only-begotten Son, who is in the bosom of the Father, he has made him known", says the Gospel of John (1:18). The Church has to make him more widely known; she has to bring men to Christ and Christ to men, so as to bring God to them and them to God. Christ is not just some great man or other with a significant religious experience; he is God, God who became man to establish a bridge between man and God so that man may become truly himself. Anyone who sees Christ only as a great religious person is not truly seeing him. The path from Christ and to Christ has to arrive at the point at which the Gospel of Mark ends up, at the confession of the Roman centurion before the Crucified One: "Truly this man was the Son of God!" (15:39). It has to arrive at the point where the Gospel of John ends up, in the confession of Thomas: "My Lord and my God!" (20:28). It has to stride along the great arch that the Gospel of Matthew sets up from the Annunciation story to the missionary speech of the Risen One. In the story of the Annunciation, Jesus is heralded as the "God with us" (1:23). And the final saying in the Gospel takes up this message: "Behold, I am with you always, to the close of the age" (28:20). In order to know Christ, we have to join in following the path along which the Gospels lead us.

The great and central task of the Church today is, as it ever was, to show people this path and to offer a pilgrim fellowship in walking it. I said just now that we know God, not simply with our understanding, but also with our will and with our heart. Therefore the knowledge of God, the knowledge of Christ, is a path that demands the involvement of the whole of our being. The most beautiful portrayal of the way we are traveling is offered by Luke in the story of the disciples going to Emmaus. This is traveling together with Christ the living Word, who interprets for us the written word, the Bible, and turns that into the path, the road along which our heart starts to burn and thus our eyes are finally opened: Scripture, the true tree of knowledge, opens our eyes for us if at the same time we are eating of Christ, the tree of life. Then we become truly able to see, and then we are truly alive. Three things belong together on this path: the fellowship of the disciples, the Scriptures, and the living presence of Christ. Thus, this journey of the disciples to Emmaus is at the same time a description of the Church—a description of how knowledge that touches on God grows and deepens. This knowledge becomes a fellowship with one another; it ends up with the Breaking of Bread, in which man becomes God's guest and God becomes man's host. Christ—it becomes clear here—is not someone we can have for ourselves alone. He leads us, not just to God, but to each other. That is why Christ and the Church belong together, just as the Church and the Bible belong together. Giving actual form to this great fellowship in the concrete individual fellowships of diocese, of parish, of ecclesial movements, is and remains the central task of the Church, yesterday, today, and tomorrow. It must become possible to experience this fellowship as a pilgrim fellowship with our cares, with the Word of God, and with Christ, and it has to lead us onward to the gift of the Sacrament, in which the marriage feast of God with mankind is ever and again anticipated.

If we look back at our reflections thus far, we can say this: the theme of Christ is ultimately not a separate, second theme beside the theme of God; rather, it is the means by which the theme of God becomes for us entirely concrete, the way it makes its presence felt, rubbing shoulders with us, as it were, and getting through to our mind. And the theme of the Church, in turn, is not a separate, third theme; rather, it is woven in support of the theme of Christ: the Church is a pilgrim fellowship with him and toward him, and it is only if she remains in this supporting role that we understand her aright; then, we can truly love her, as one loves companions on a journey.

The individual elements of this traveling ought actually now to be expounded in somewhat more detail. Pope John Paul II, in his apostolic letter *Novo millennio ineunte*, has said everything that is essential on this subject, so in the closing part of these reflections I should like to make do with a couple of footnotes to this. In this text the pope speaks at length about the meaning of prayer, which is what really makes the Christian a Christian. In prayer, he says, we experience the primacy of grace: God is always there before us. Christianity is not moralism, not our own construct. First, God moves to meet us, and then we can go along with him; our inner powers are freed. And prayer, he continues, makes it possible for us to experience the primacy of Christ, the primacy of inwardness and of holiness. At this point the pope adds a question well worth pondering: "When this principle is not respected, is it any wonder that pastoral plans come to nothing and leave us with a disheartening sense of frustration?" (no. 38). Over and above all our activism, we have to learn anew the primacy of inwardness—the mystical component of Christianity has to gain renewed force.

From personal prayer, the pope quite logically moves on to shared liturgical prayer, above all to the Sunday Eucharist. Sunday, as the day of the Resurrection, and the Eucharist, as a meeting with the Risen One, belong together. Time needs to have its inner rhythm. It needs the correspondence

between the everyday period of our work and the solemn
encounter with Christ in church, in the Sacrament. The
pope quite rightly views winning back Sunday as a pastoral
task of the first order. In that way, time is given its inner
ordering; God once more becomes the starting point of
time and the point at which it is aiming. This is also at the
same time the day of human fellowship, the family's day (on
a small scale), and also the day on which the great family, the
family of God, takes form in the Church and the Church
becomes something we experience. If anyone knows the
Church only from committee sessions and papers, he does
not know her. Then she becomes an offense, because either
she becomes the object of our own constructive activities,
or she appears as something imposed upon us from outside,
something alien. We know the Church from within only if
we experience her at that moment when she is transcending herself, when the Lord enters into her and makes her
his dwelling and, thereby, makes us his brothers and sisters.
That is why the dignified celebration of the Eucharist is so
important, a celebration in which the Church's dispossess-
sion of herself must appear. We do not make the liturgy
ourselves. We do not think something up, as secular festival committees do, or in the way that quizmasters proudly
present something. The Lord comes. The liturgy derives
from him, has grown up from the apostles in the faith of
the Church; we enter into it; we do not construct it. That
is the only way there can be celebration, and celebration—
as an anticipation of future freedom—is essential for man.
We could go so far as to say: this is the Church's task, to
vouchsafe us the experience of celebration. Celebration,
festivals, have arisen throughout the whole history of mankind as cultic events and are unthinkable without the divine
presence. Celebration attains its full stature when God truly
becomes our guest and invites us to share in his banquet.

There are two more points I should like to mention. The pope moves on from the Sunday liturgy to the Sacrament of Reconciliation. No sacrament has become so alien to us, in recent decades, as this one has. And yet, who could fail to be aware that we need reconciliation? That we have a need for forgiveness, for inner cleansing? Meanwhile, we have switched to psychotherapy and psychoanalysis, and I would not quarrel with their tasks or their capacities. Yet without the word of reconciliation that comes from God, our attempts to repair sick spirits remain inadequate. That leads me to a second comment. I had said that the whole of man is required for the knowledge of God—understanding, will, and heart. In practice, this means that we cannot know God unless we are prepared to accept his will, to take it as the measure and the orientation for our lives. In still more practical terms, that means that living in accordance with the Commandments is a part of belonging to the pilgrim fellowship of faith, the fellowship of those traveling toward God. This is not a heteronomous rule being imposed upon man. It is in assenting to the will of God that our being made truly similar to God is actually effected and we become what we are: the image of God. And because God is love, that is why the Commandments, in which his will is made known, are the essential variations of the single theme of love. They are the practical rules of love for God, for my neighbor, for creation, for ourselves. And because, again, there exists in Christ the entire assent to God's will, the full stature of being in God's image, living in accordance with love and within the will of God means following Christ, moving toward him and walking together with him.

Reference to the Commandments has become quite muted, even in the Church, in the last few decades;

suspicion of legalism and moralism has risen so high. And indeed, what the Commandments say remains external if it is not illuminated by the inwardness of God within us and by the way Christ has gone ahead on behalf of us all. It remains moralistic if it is not standing in the light of the grace of forgiveness. Israel was proud of knowing God's will and, thus, knowing the way of life. Psalm 119 as a whole is an ever-repeated outbreak of joy and thankfulness at knowing God's will. We know this will now as having become flesh in Jesus Christ, showing us the way and at the same time showing compassion, time and again picking us up and leading us on. Should we not rejoice anew for this, in the midst of a world filled with darkness and confusion? The reawakening of joy in God, joy in God's revelation and in friendship with God, seems to me an urgent task for the Church in our century. For us, too, in particular, the saying is true that Ezra the priest cried out to the people of Israel when their courage had ebbed after the exile: "The joy of the LORD is your strength" (Neh 8:10).

I should like to close with an image from Dante's *Divine Comedy*. We started from the descent into hell into a world without God. Dante portrays the path of purification, the way to God, as the ascent of a mountain. The external path becomes a symbol of the inner way to the real heights, the heights of God. At first, the climbing becomes infinitely difficult for the earth-bound man. In Dante's poetic vision, after the first stage of the path, an angel blots out from the climber's forehead the sign of pride, and now a strange feeling comes over him as he pursues his way: "Already we were mounting up the holy cliffs, and to me it was as if I had become far lighter than I had felt myself to be previously, on level ground. So I spoke: 'Master, say, what heavy load has been taken from me, that it scarcely feels much trouble when I walk, any more'"? (*Purgatorio*, canto 12, ll. 115–20). Being freed from pride means being able to overcome our difficulties. Our own thoughts, such as arrogance, greed, ambition, and whatever else dark and evil there is dwelling in our souls—these are like lead weights that hinder our upward climb, that make us unable to reach the heights. "The purer man becomes, the more closely is he related to him who is above. He loses weight, he has more strength for climbing.... Freedom grows; it is complete when the will becomes one with the demand."[2] The pilgrim fellowship of faith, which we call the Church, should be a fellowship in climbing, a fellowship in which those processes of cleansing are effected in us that render us capable of the true heights of human existence, of fellowship with God. In the same measure as we are cleansed, the climbing, which is at first so difficult, rapidly becomes a joy. This joy must more and more shine forth from the Church into the world.

---

[2] Romano Guardini, *Der Engel in Dantes Göttlicher Komödie* [The angel in Dante's *Divine Comedy*], 3rd ed. (Mainz and Paderborn: Matthias-Grünewald-Verlag, 1995), 48–49.

V

An Ever-Reforming Society

Speech at the Rimini Meeting
for Friendship among Peoples,
September 1, 1990

Dear friends! Thank you for your very warm welcome!
You know the title of my lecture: "An Ever-Reforming
Society".

It doesn't take much imagination to guess that the society of which I wish to speak is the Church. Perhaps the
word *Church* is omitted in the title only because it would
spontaneously provoke a defensive reaction in most
people today. They think, "We have heard too much
about the Church, and what we hear is not pleasant at
all." The word and the reality of the Church have fallen
into discredit. And so, it is thought, even a permanent,
continuous reform will not change anything. Or perhaps, the problem is that up till now, we have not found
out what kind of reform could make the Church into a
society that is truly worth living in. Let us ask above all:
Why is the Church looked on with such disfavor by so

Translated by Teresa Benedetta for the International Association for the
Preservation of the Heritage of Benedict XVI (Papst Press). Translation modified for style by Ignatius Press.

many people, even among believers, even among those who, up till yesterday, one could consider some of the most faithful or who, despite suffering, still are faithful in some way today?

The reasons are very diverse, sometimes even contradictory, depending on the positions taken. Some suffer because the Church has adapted too much to the parameters of today's world. Others are annoyed because they consider her still too alienated from the world. For the most part, the discontent with the Church starts with the fact that she seems to be an institution like so many others, and as such, she is seen as limiting one's personal freedom. The thirst for freedom is the form that today expresses the desire for liberation, the perception of not being free, of being alienated. Invoking freedom expresses an aspiration to an existence that is not limited by what is given—which would hinder my full personal development by presenting me from the outside with the road that I should follow. But everywhere, one comes across barriers and roadblocks of this type that bring us to a halt and prevent us from going farther. Thus, any barriers that the Church raises are seen as doubly heavy, because they penetrate into our most personal and intimate sphere. But the norms of the Church are far more than traffic rules aimed at minimizing confrontations during human coexistence. These rules have to do with my interior course—they tell me how I should interpret and configure my freedom. These rules require that I make decisions, which cannot always be done without the pain of renouncing something. But do they not perhaps mean to deny us the best fruits in the garden? Is it not true that the constraints of so many commandments and prohibitions do bar the way to an open horizon? And does all this not hinder thought and will from greatness?

Should not liberation consist in getting out from under such spiritual guidance? And is not the one true reform perhaps to reject all such rules? Well, then, what would remain of this "society"?

Bitterness against the Church also has a specific reason. In fact, in a world that is governed by hard discipline and inexorable constrictions, a silent hope continues to be directed at the Church: that she can represent a small island of a better life, a small oasis of freedom to which one may retreat from time to time. Anger against the Church or disappointment in her therefore has a specific character, because tacitly, more is expected of her than of worldly institutions—the silent hope that in the Church, the dream of a better life can be realized. Therefore, how much more one would wish to experience within her that taste of liberty, of being free, of leaving the cave, as Gregory the Great said, drawing from Plato.

Nonetheless, the moment that the Church, in her concrete aspect, becomes so far removed from such a dream, and takes on the flavor of a worldly institution and everything that is merely human, she becomes the target of particularly bitter anger. And this anger cannot be less, if only because those who had placed their hopes in her cannot extinguish their dream. Since the Church is not as she appears in their dreams, they seek desperately to make her over into what they want her to be: a place where one may express all freedoms, a space in which our limits can be surpassed, where one may experience that utopia that has to be somewhere. As in the field of political activity, they would wish finally to build a better world, or they think that there should finally be a better Church—or at least, the first step toward one: a Church that is fully human, full of fraternity, of generous creativity, a dwelling of reconciliation among all and for all.

Useless Reform

But how should this come about? How can such a reform be carried out?

Well, we must begin somewhere, it is said—often with the ingenuous presumption of the enlightened, who are convinced that the generations up to now never really understood the problem, or that they were too fearful and unenlightened. Today, it is thought, we finally have both courage and intelligence, and for all the resistance that reactionaries and "fundamentalists" may oppose to this noble undertaking, it must be set into motion. That, at least, is the formula of the "enlightened" for the first step.

The Church is not a democracy. Since she first appeared, she has not integrated into her internal constitution that patrimony of rights and freedoms that the Enlightenment elaborated and that have since been recognized as the fundamental rules for sociopolitical formation. Thus it seems like the most normal thing in the world to recover once and for all whatever had been obscured or neglected in the past, and to start setting up this fundamental patrimony of structures of freedom. The path would lead, as they like to say, from a paternalistic Church that dispenses goods to a Church that is a community. They say that no one should be just a passive receiver of the good that makes one a Christian. Instead, everyone must become an active operator in Christian life, and the Church should never again be seen as coming down from on high. No! It is we who "make" the Church, and we shall see to it that she will always be new. That way, she will finally become "our" Church, and we shall be her active, responsible subjects. The passive aspect yields to the active. The Church will arise through discussions, agreements, and decisions. In the debate there emerges that which can be demanded still today, that which can still today be recognized by all as belonging to the faith, or as an orienting moral guideline. New, abbreviated "formulas of faith" will be coined. In Germany, at a fairly high level, it has been said that even the liturgy should no longer correspond to a prescribed rubric, but rather should just emerge on site, as needed—in a specific situation, and determined by the community for which it is being celebrated. And even that improvisation should have nothing previously constituted—it should be something entirely self-generated, as an expression of the moment. In this, the words of Scripture would be seen as something of a hindrance, even if they cannot be completely renounced. One could say one faces a great freedom of choice. But there are not many scriptural texts that can be adapted without "disturbing" that ideal of "self-realization" to which, it now seems, liturgy is destined.

But in this work of reform, during which finally, it is said, even in the Church "self-determination" or "self-management" will replace being guided by others, questions promptly arise. Who exactly is responsible for making decisions? And on what basis are these decisions made? In the political democracy, this question is answered by a system of representation: individuals choose a representative, who then makes the decisions for them. This responsibility is limited in time; it is circumscribed even by the party system, and encompasses only those fields of political action specifically assigned by the constitution. But even in this respect, questions remain: the minority must bow to the majority, even if this minority can be quite large. Besides, it is not guaranteed that the representative I have elected necessarily acts and speaks the way I wish. Thus, when we look at it more closely, even the victorious majority cannot in fact consider themselves entirely active subjects in political events. On the contrary, they must accept even "decisions made by others", if only not to endanger the democratic system in its entirety.

But more important for us is a more general problem. Everything that men do can likewise be nullified by others. Everything that comes from human taste will not necessarily please everybody. Everything that a majority decides can later be abrogated by another majority. And so a Church that depends on the decisions of a majority becomes a Church that is purely human. She becomes reduced to something doable and plausible, to the fruits of her own actions, intuitions, and opinions. Opinion takes the place of faith. Indeed, in the coined "professions of faith" that I am familiar with, the meaning of the expression *credo*—"I believe"—does not go beyond "This is what we think." The "self-made" Church is ultimately "just herself", and others who are "just themselves" may never like this "just herself" Church, which soon reveals her own smallness. She would retreat to the field of the empirical and, in this way, cease to be even the ideal that was dreamed about.

The Nature of True Reform

The activist—who wants to do everything himself—is the opposite of the person who admires. The activist restricts the field of his own reason and thus loses sight of mystery. The more the Church extends the range of things that people decide for themselves and do for themselves, the narrower she becomes for all of us. The great and liberating dimension of the Church is not in what we ourselves do but in that which is given to all of us—that which does not come from our own will and invention, but from something that precedes us, something that comes to us from an unimaginable source, a source "greater than our heart". Reformation, which is necessary in every age, does not consist in the fact that we can remodel "our Church" anew all the time as it would please us, or that we can invent her, but rather that we constantly clear away our own personal constructs, in favor of the most pure light that comes from above, which is also the irruption of pure freedom.

Let me explain what I mean with an image, which I take from Michelangelo, who for his part has taken it from ancient concepts of Christian mysticism and philosophy. With his artist's vision, Michelangelo saw in the stone before him the image hidden beneath, waiting to be liberated and brought to light. The task of the artist, in his view, was simply to take away that which still covered that image. Michelangelo thought of authentic artistic activity as bringing something to light, releasing it, not "making" it.

The same idea applied to anthropology was already evident in Saint Bonaventure, who explained the journey through which man becomes authentically himself by using the image of the sculptor. The sculptor doesn't "make" something, explained the great Franciscan theologian. Instead, his work is an *ablatio*—which consists of eliminating, of trimming away what is not authentic. Thus, through *ablatio*, the *forma nobilis* emerges, the precious figure. Thus it is for man: so that the image of God may shine in him, he must above all, and first of all, welcome that purification through which the sculptor, namely God, frees him from all the debris that obscures the authentic aspect of his being, that makes him appear as nothing more than a gross block of stone, when really the divine image dwells in him.

If we understand it correctly, we can also find in this image the model and guide for ecclesial reform. Of course, the Church will always need new human structures to support her, in order that she may speak and function in every historical epoch. Such ecclesial structures and institutions, with their juridical configurations, far from being something evil, are, on the contrary, simply necessary and indispensable. But institutions age, and they risk presenting themselves as essential, thus distracting from what is really and truly essential. That is why institutions must always be "removed" like scaffolding that has become superfluous. Reform is always a new *ablatio*—a trimming off, so that the *forma nobilis* may emerge once more: the face of the Bride, and with it, the face of the Bridegroom himself, the living Lord. A similar *ablatio*, a "negative theology", is a way toward a goal that is all positive. Only thus can the Divine penetrate, and only thus can there emerge a *congregatio*—an assembly, a gathering, a purification, that pure community that we yearn for—a community in which the "I" is no longer against another "I", a "self" no longer against another "self". Rather, self-giving, that trusting abandonment which is part of love, becomes the reciprocal receiving of all that is good and all that is pure. Thus, for each of us, the word of the generous father applies, who reminds his envious son of what is contained in every freedom and every utopia that is realized: "All that is mine is yours" (Lk 15:31; cf. Jn 17:1ff).

Once again, true reform is *ablatio*, which, as such, becomes *congregatio*. Let us try to grasp this basic idea in a more concrete way. In a first approach, we opposed the activist to the admirer, and we decided in favor of the latter. But what exactly does their opposition mean? The activist, who always wants to be doing something, places his own activity above everything. This limits his horizon to only that which is doable, to what can become an object of his doing. Properly speaking, all he sees are objects. He is not, in fact, capable of seeing anything bigger than he is, because that could set a limit to what he can do. So he restricts the world to only that which is empirical. Man cuts himself off. And the activist builds his own prison, against which he himself will later protest to high heaven.

Instead, true wonder says no to this restriction to the empirical, to the mere here and now. True wonder prepares man for an act of faith that opens wide before him the horizon of the Eternal. Only the Eternal has no limits and is sufficiently wide for our nature, because only the unlimited is adequate to our calling as human beings in the likeness of God. Where this horizon disappears, every residue of freedom becomes too small, and all freedoms that can be subsequently proposed are an insipid surrogate that will never suffice. The first fundamental *ablatio* that is necessary for the Church is always the act of faith itself—that act of faith that rips the barrier of the finite and opens up space for reaching out to the limitless. Faith leads us a long way, into limitless lands, as the Psalms say. Modern scientific thinking has increasingly caged us within the prison of positivism and has thus condemned us to pragmatism. Through it, many things can be achieved. We can even travel to the moon and beyond in the limitlessness of the cosmos.

Notwithstanding all this, we remain at the same point, because we cannot go beyond the frontier of the quantifiable and the doable.

Albert Camus described the absurdity of this form of freedom in the figure of the emperor Caligula. Everything was at his disposal, and yet everything was too narrow for him. In his mad desire to have increasingly more, increasingly greater things, he cried out: "I want the moon, give me the moon!" Meanwhile, it has become possible for us to have the moon in some way. But until the true and real frontier opens, the frontier between Heaven and earth, between God and the world, even the moon is simply another piece of ground, and reaching it does not bring us a step closer to the freedom and fullness that we desire.

The fundamental liberation that the Church can give herself is to stay in the horizon of the Eternal, to leave the limits of our knowledge and power. Faith itself, in all its greatness and amplitude, is therefore the constant essential reform that we need. Starting with the faith, we must always put to the test those institutions that we ourselves have made in the Church. This means that the Church must be the bridge of faith, and that she—especially in her associations within the world—cannot be an end in herself. The notion has become widespread, even in high Church circles, that a person is more Christian the more he is involved in Church activities. There is an urge toward a kind of ecclesiastical therapy by activity, to make work—to try to assign everyone to some committee, or at any rate, some task within the Church. Somehow, so they think, there must always be some ecclesial activity. One must always talk about the Church, one must always do something for her or in her. But a mirror that reflects nothing but itself is no longer a mirror. It is no longer a window that allows looking toward a farther horizon, but it becomes a screen between the observer and the world, and therefore has lost its sense. It may happen that someone uninterruptedly exercises ecclesial activities but is not necessarily Christian—just as someone could simply live from the Word and the sacraments and practice the love that comes from faith without ever being part of a Church committee, never bothering about developments in Church politics, never taking part in synods or voting in one, and yet be a true Christian.

We need not a more human Church but a more divine one, because only then can she be truly human. Thus it is that everything done by man within the Church should be recognized for the service that it is, but it must take its place behind what really counts and what is essential. Freedom, which we reasonably expect from the Church and in the Church, is not realized by applying the principle of majority rule. It does not depend on the fact that the widest possible majority must prevail over the narrowest possible minority. Rather, it depends on the fact that no one can impose his own will on others, but that everyone must acknowledge being bound to the word and the will of the Only One who is our Lord and our freedom. The atmosphere becomes closed and suffocating in the Church if the bearers of its ministry forget that the sacrament is not a distribution of power, but rather an appropriation of the self, of myself, in favor of him in whose person I as a priest must speak and act. Wherever greater responsibility corresponds to ever greater self-expropriation, then no one is a slave to another. The Lord dominates, and thus the principle that the Lord is the Spirit, "and where the Spirit of the Lord is, there is freedom" (2 Cor 3:17).

The more apparatuses we construct, even the most up-to-date, the less space we have for the Spirit, the less space we have for the Lord, and the less freedom we have. I think that we should, from this viewpoint, initiate in the Church at all levels an examination of conscience without reservations. At all levels, this examination of conscience should have sufficiently concrete consequences, and bring with it an *ablatio* that will allow the true face of the Church to appear once more. This could give back to all of us a sense of freedom, and allow us to find ourselves at home in the Church in a completely new way.

Morality, Forgiveness, and Expiation: The Personal Center of Reform

Let us look briefly, before proceeding further, at what we have brought to light so far. First, we spoke of a double "cutting away", of an act of liberation that is twofold: an act of purification and of renewal. We touched on the faith that can break down the wall of the finite and can free our vision toward the dimensions of the Eternal—not only our vision, but also the path. Faith is not just knowing and acknowledging, but a functioning. It is not just a break in the wall, but a hand that saves, that draws us out of the cave. From this, we drew the consequences for institutions, in that the essential basic order of the Church always needs new concrete developments and concrete configurations, but these configurations cannot become the essential thing. Indeed, the Church does not exist for the purpose of keeping us all occupied like any other worldly association, nor of keeping herself alive as such. She exists to be for all of us the access to eternal life.

Now we must take the next step and apply all these reflections not only in the general and objective sense, as we have done till now, but personally. In fact, even here in the personal sphere, it is also necessary to effect a trimming off that liberates us. On the personal level, it will not always be the *forma nobilis*, that is, the image of God inscribed in us, that will leap to the eye. Instead, we see ourselves as the image of Adam, of a man who is not totally ruined but nonetheless degraded. We can see the incrustations of dust and filth that overlie the image. We all need the true Sculptor who will cut off all that distorts the image. We need forgiveness, which constitutes the nucleus of every true reform. It was certainly not by chance that in the three decisive stages of the Church's formation, as told by the

Gospels, the remission of sins plays an essential role. First, when Jesus entrusted the keys to Peter, the power given to him to bind and unbind, to open and close—which is what we speak of with regard to sins—is, at its core, a charge to allow entry, to give a welcome home, to forgive (Mt 16:19). We find the same thing at the Last Supper, which inaugurated the new community based on the Body of Christ, and in the Body of Christ. It became possible from the fact that the Lord shed his blood "for many for the forgiveness of sins" (Mt 26:28). Finally, the Risen Lord, in his first appearance to the Eleven, founds the communion of his peace on the fact that he gives them the power to forgive (Jn 20:19–23). The Church is not a community of "people who do not need doctors", but rather a community of converted sinners, who live on the grace of forgiveness, transmitting it in turn to others.

If we read the New Testament carefully, we discover that forgiveness in itself has nothing magic about it; but neither is it a pretense of forgetting, of "pretending it didn't happen". Rather, it is a process of change that is very real, one that the Sculptor accomplishes. When sin is taken away, something is really removed, and the advent of forgiveness is revealed by the penitence that follows. In this sense, forgiveness is both an active and a passive process: the powerful creative word of God brings upon us the pain of change, which becomes an active transformation. Forgiveness and penitence, grace and personal conversion, are not contradictory, but two faces of one and the same event. This fusion of activity and passivity expresses the essential form of human existence. Indeed, all our "creating" starts with our being creatures, with our participation in the creative activity of God.

And here we come to a truly central point: I believe that the spiritual crisis of our time has its roots in the obscuring of the grace of forgiveness. But let us first observe the positive aspect of the present: the moral dimension is beginning to be held up anew little by little. It is being acknowledged—or rather, it has become evident—that every technical progress is questionable and ultimately destructive if each step forward does not also correspond to a moral growth. It is recognized that there cannot be a reform of men and of mankind without moral renewal. But the invocation of morality remains ultimately listless and weak, because its parameters are hidden behind a dense cloud of debate. In effect, man cannot abide pure and simple moralism—he cannot live with it. It becomes for him a "law" that provokes his desire to contradict it, and thus generates sin....

In general terms, one can say that moral discussion today tends to liberate men from blame, to the point of making sure that the conditions for its possibility never enter into the discussion. One is reminded of a mordant expression from Pascal: "Ecce patres, qui tollunt peccata mundi!": "Behold the fathers who take away the sins of the world." According to these "moralists", there is simply no blame anymore. Naturally, this way of freeing the world from blame is much too cheap. Within themselves, the men who are thus "liberated" know quite well that all this is not true, that there is sin, that they themselves are sinners, and that there must be an effective way to overcome sin. Jesus himself did not call to himself those who had already been liberated on their own and who therefore believed they had no need of him, but those who knew themselves to be sinners who therefore did need him.

Morality preserves its own gravity only if there is forgiveness, true forgiveness that is effective. Otherwise, it falls into pure and empty conditionalism. True forgiveness only comes at a price, "an equitable exchange rate", if the sin is expiated, if there is expiation. The circle of morality-forgiveness-expiation cannot be broken up: if one element is missing, everything falls apart. The undivided nature of this circle determines whether there is redemption for man or not. In the Torah—the five books of Moses—these three elements are indivisibly tied to each other, and it is therefore not possible to extract a moral law that is always valid from this central covenant of the canon of the Old Testament, as the Enlightenment thinkers did, while abandoning the rest of it to history. This moralistic modality of interpreting the Old Testament necessarily ends in failure. This was precisely the error made by Pelagius, who has more followers today than one might think at first glance. Instead, Jesus fulfilled the whole Law, not just a part of it, and therefore, he renewed it from the base. He himself, who suffered in expiating every human sin, is expiation and forgiveness contemporaneously, and is thus the only sure and always valid basis for our morality.

One cannot dissociate morality from Christology, because it cannot be separated from expiation and forgiveness. In Christ, every part of the Law is fulfilled, and therefore, morality becomes for us a true and fulfillable exigency. Starting with the nucleus of faith, then, the way to renewal is always open for the individual, for the Church in her entirety, and for mankind.

Suffering, Martyrdom, and the Joy of Redemption

There is much to say about this. But I will try, very briefly, to emphasize once more, in conclusion, that which seems to be most important in our context. Forgiveness and its realization in myself, through penitence and its consequences, is in the first place the center of everything personal in any renewal. But precisely because forgiveness concerns the individual in his most intimate nucleus, he is capable of accepting it integrally, and he can become a center of renewal for the larger community. If, in fact, the dust and the filth are cleaned away that had made me unrecognizable as an image of God, then I am not different from my neighbor, who is also an image of God. Above all, I become similar to Christ, who is the human image of God without any limitations whatsoever, the model upon which all of us were created. Paul expresses this process in rather extreme terms: "The old has passed away, behold, the new has come" (2 Cor 5:17), and "It is no longer I who live, but Christ who lives in me" (Gal 2:20). It is a process of death and rebirth—I am torn away from my isolation and am received into a new community-subject: my "I" is inserted into the "I" of Christ and is thus united to that of all my brothers. Only from the profundity of such a renewal of the individual is the Church born—the community that unites and sustains in life and in death. Only when we take all this into consideration will we see the Church in her correct order of magnitude.

The Church is not only the small group of activists who find themselves together at a certain place to initiate a communitarian life. Nor is she simply the great host of those who gather together on Sundays to celebrate the Eucharist. Finally, the Church is also much more than the pope, bishops, and priests, those who are invested with the sacramental ministry. All these whom we have named are part of the Church, but the radius of the society that we join through faith extends far beyond that, even beyond death. All the saints, beginning with Abel and Abraham, are part of her, along with all the witnesses to hope that the Old Testament recounts, and Mary, Mother of the Lord, and his apostles, down to Thomas Becket and Thomas More, to Maximilian

Kolbe, Edith Stein, and Pier Giorgio Frassati. And so are all the unknowns and the unnamed, whose faith no one has known except God, the men and women in all places and all times whose hearts reached to Christ with hope and love, to the "pioneer and perfecter of our faith", as the letter to the Hebrews calls him (12:2).

It is not the occasional majorities that form here and there in the Church who decide her path and ours. The saints are the true determining majority according to which we orient ourselves. It is to them that we look! They have translated the divine into the human, the eternal into time. They are our teachers in humanity, who do not abandon us in pain and in solitude, but even at the hour of death are there beside us.

Here we touch on something very important. A vision of the world that cannot give meaning to pain and make it precious does not serve for anything. It fails precisely where the decisive question of existence arises. Those who have nothing else to say about pain but that we should fight it are deluding us. Of course we should do everything to alleviate the pain of so many innocents and to minimize suffering. But there is no human life without pain, and whoever is incapable of accepting pain excludes himself from that purification which alone can make us mature. In communion with Christ, pain becomes full of significance, not only for me, as a process of *ablatio*, in which God strips from me the debris that obscures his image, but beyond me, useful for everyone, so that we can all say with Saint Paul, "Now I rejoice in my sufferings for your sake, and in my flesh I complete what is lacking in Christ's afflictions for the sake of his body, that is, the Church" (Col 1:24). Thomas Becket—who together with Einstein and the figure of the Admirer has been our guide in our reflections these days—encourages us to take a further step. Life goes far beyond our biological existence. When there is no reason that is worth dying for, then life itself is not worth living. Where faith has opened our eyes and made our heart larger, then another expression from Saint Paul acquires all its power of illumination: "None of us lives to himself, and none of us dies to himself. If we live, we live to the Lord, and if we die, we die to the Lord; so then, whether we live or whether we die, we are the Lord's" (Rom 14:7–8). The more we are rooted in the society of Jesus Christ and all those who belong to him, the more our life shall be sustained by that irradiating trust to which Saint Paul also gave expression: "For I am sure that neither death, nor life, nor angels, nor principalities, nor things present, nor things to come, nor powers, nor height, nor depth, nor anything else in all creation, will be able to separate us from the love of God in Christ Jesus our Lord" (Rom 8:38–39).

Dear friends, it is with such faith that we should allow ourselves to be filled! Then the Church will grow as communion in our journey within true life, and she will renew herself day by day. Then she will become the great house with many dwellings. Then the multiplicity of the Holy Spirit's gifts can work within her. Then we shall see "how good and how pleasant it is when brothers dwell in unity ... like the dew of Hermon, which falls on the mountains of Zion! For there, the LORD has commanded the blessing, life for evermore" (Ps 133:1–3).

VI

Liturgy: God Takes First Place

Preface to the Russian-language edition of
Theology of the Liturgy, volume 11 of
Ratzinger's *Collected Works*

Nihil Operi Dei praeponatur, let nothing be preferred before
the Work of God. With these words, Saint Benedict, in
his *Rule* (43.3), established the absolute priority of Divine
Worship over every other duty of the monastic life. This
maxim, even in the monastic life, did not turn out to be
immediately obvious, because for the monks their work
in agriculture and in learning was also an essential duty.
Both in agriculture and also in handicrafts and in the work
of formation there could certainly be pressing temporal
matters that might appear to be more important than the
liturgy. Faced with all this, Benedict, in assigning priority
to the liturgy, unequivocally highlights the priority of God
himself in our life: "At the hour of Divine Office, as soon
as the signal has been heard, let the monk leave whatever
he may have in hand and make great haste, but with due
gravity" (43.1).

In the consciousness of people nowadays, the things of
God and, consequently, the liturgy do not appear urgent at
all. Every possible thing has its urgency. God's cause seems
never to be urgent. Now, it could be argued that monastic

life is in any case something different from the life of men and women in the world, and this is of course right. And yet the priority of God that we have forgotten is true for everyone. If God is no longer important, the criteria for deciding what is important shift. In setting God aside, man subjects himself to constraints that make him the slave of material forces and that thus are opposed to his dignity.

In the years following the Second Vatican Council, I became conscious once again of the priority of God and of the Divine Liturgy. The misunderstanding of the liturgical reform that spread widely in the Catholic Church led to an increasing prominence of the aspect of instruction and of one's own activity and creativity. The doings of men almost made us forget the presence of God. In such a situation, it became increasingly clear that the existence of the Church is vitally dependent on the correct celebration of the liturgy and that the Church is in danger when the primacy of God no longer appears in the liturgy and thus in life. The most profound reason for the crisis that upset the Church lies in the eclipse of God's priority in the liturgy. All this led me to dedicate myself to the theme of the liturgy more extensively than in the past, because I knew that the true renewal of the liturgy is a fundamental prerequisite for the renewal of the Church. The studies that are collected in the present volume XI of the *Collected Writings* originated on the basis of this conviction. But fundamentally, even with all the differences, the essence of the liturgy is one and the same in the East and the West. And so I hope that this book may help the Christians of Russia also to understand in a new and better way the great gift that is given to us in the Sacred Liturgy.

VII

The Sacred Character of the Eucharist

Homily for the Solemnity of Corpus Christi,
June 7, 2012

Dear brothers and sisters,

This evening I would like to meditate with you on two interconnected aspects of the Eucharistic Mystery: worship of the Eucharist and its sacred nature. It is important to reflect on them once again to preserve them from incomplete visions of the Mystery itself, such as those encountered in the recent past.

First of all, a reflection on the importance of Eucharistic worship and, in particular, adoration of the Blessed Sacrament. We shall experience it this evening, after Mass, before the procession, during it, and at its conclusion. A unilateral interpretation of the Second Vatican Council penalized this dimension, in practice restricting the Eucharist to the moment of its celebration. Indeed, it was very important to recognize the centrality of the celebration in which the Lord summons his people, gathers it round the dual table of the Word and of the Bread of Life, nourishes and unites it with himself in the offering of the Sacrifice.

Of course, this evaluation of the liturgical assembly in which the Lord works his mystery of communion and brings it about still applies; but it must be put back into the proper balance. In fact—as often happens—in order to emphasize one aspect, one ends by sacrificing another. In this case, the correct accentuation of the celebration of the Eucharist has been to the detriment of adoration as an act of faith and prayer addressed to the Lord Jesus, really present in the Sacrament of the Altar.

This imbalance has also had repercussions on the spiritual life of the faithful. In fact, by concentrating the entire relationship with the Eucharistic Jesus in the sole moment of Holy Mass, one risks emptying the rest of existential time and space of his presence. This makes ever less perceptible the meaning of Jesus' constant presence in our midst and with us, a presence that is tangible, close, in our homes, as the "beating Heart" of the city, of the country, and of the area, with its various expressions and activities. The sacrament of Christ's charity must permeate the whole of daily life.

Actually, it is wrong to set celebration and adoration against each other, as if they were competing. Exactly the opposite is true: worship of the Blessed Sacrament is, as it were, the spiritual "context" in which the community can celebrate the Eucharist well and in truth. Only if it is preceded, accompanied, and followed by this inner attitude of faith and adoration can the liturgical action express its full meaning and value. The encounter with Jesus in Holy Mass is truly and fully brought about when the community can recognize that in the Sacrament he dwells in his house, waits for us, invites us to his table, then, after the assembly is dismissed, stays with us, with his discreet and silent presence, and accompanies us with his intercession, continuing to gather our spiritual sacrifices and offer them to the Father.

In this regard, I am pleased to highlight the experience we shall be having together this evening, too. At the moment of adoration, we are all equal, kneeling before the Sacrament of Love. The common priesthood and the ministerial priesthood are brought together in Eucharistic worship. It is a very beautiful and significant experience that we have had several times in Saint Peter's Basilica and also in the unforgettable Vigils with young people—I recall, for example, those in Cologne, London, Zagreb, and Madrid. It is clear to all that these moments of Eucharistic Vigil prepare for the celebration of the Holy Mass, they prepare hearts for the encounter so that it will be more fruitful.

To be all together in prolonged silence before the Lord present in his Sacrament is one of the most genuine experiences of our being Church, which is accompanied complementarily by the celebration of the Eucharist, by listening to the Word of God, by singing, and by approaching the table of the Bread of Life together. Communion and contemplation cannot be separated; they go hand in hand. If I am truly to communicate with another person, I must know him, I must be able to be in silence close to him, to listen to him and look at him lovingly. True love and true friendship are always nourished by the reciprocity of looks, of intense, eloquent silences full of respect and veneration, so that the encounter may be lived profoundly and personally rather than superficially. And, unfortunately, if this dimension is lacking, sacramental Communion itself may become a superficial gesture on our part.

Instead, in true Communion, prepared for by the conversation of prayer and of life, we can address words of confidence to the Lord, such as those that rang out just now in the Responsorial Psalm: "O LORD, I am your servant; I am your servant, the son of your handmaid. / You have loosed my bonds. / I will offer to you the sacrifice of thanksgiving / and call on the name of the LORD" (Ps 116:16–17).

I would now like to move on briefly to the second aspect: the sacred nature of the Eucharist. Here, too, we have heard in the recent past of a certain misunderstanding of the authentic message of Sacred Scripture. The Christian novelty with regard to worship has been influenced by a certain secularist mentality of the 1960s and '70s. It is true—and this is still the case—that the center of worship is now no longer in the ancient rites and sacrifices, but in Christ himself, in his person, in his life, in his Paschal Mystery. However, it must be concluded from this fundamental innovation, not that the sacred no longer exists, but rather that it has found fulfillment in Jesus Christ, divine Love incarnate.

The Letter to the Hebrews, which we heard this evening in the second reading, speaks to us precisely of the newness of the priesthood of Christ, "high priest of the good things that have come" (Heb 9:11), but does not say that the priesthood is finished. Christ "is the mediator of a new covenant" (Heb 9:15), established in his blood that purifies our "conscience from dead works" (Heb 9:14). He did not abolish the sacred but brought it to fulfillment, inaugurating a new form of worship, which is indeed fully spiritual but which, however, as long as we are journeying in time, still makes use of signs and rites, which will exist no longer only at the end, in the heavenly Jerusalem, where there will no longer be any temple (cf. Rev 21:22). Thanks to Christ, the sacred is truer, more intense, and, as happens with the Commandments, also more demanding! Ritual observance does not suffice, but purification of the heart and the involvement of one's life are required.

I would also like to stress that the sacred has an educational function, and its disappearance inevitably impoverishes culture and especially the formation of the new generations. If, for example, in the name of a faith that is secularized and no longer in need of sacred signs, these Corpus Christi processions through the city were to be abolished, the spiritual profile of Rome would be "flattened out", and our personal and community awareness would be weakened.

Or let us think of a mother or father who, in the name of a desacralized faith, deprived their children of all religious rituals: in reality, they would end by giving a free hand to the many substitutes that exist in the consumer society, to other rites and other signs that could more easily become idols.

God, our Father, did not do this with humanity: he sent his Son into the world, not to abolish, but to give fulfillment also to the sacred. At the height of this mission, at the Last Supper, Jesus instituted the Sacrament of his Body and his Blood, the Memorial of his Paschal Sacrifice. By so doing, he replaced the ancient sacrifices with himself, but he did so in a rite that he commanded the apostles to perpetuate, as a supreme sign of the true Sacred One who is he himself. With this faith, dear brothers and sisters, let us celebrate the Eucharistic Mystery today and every day and adore it as the center of our lives and the heart of the world. Amen.

VIII

I Would Like to Be with You Always

Meeting with Children Who Have Received Their First Communion, October 15, 2005

Andrea: Dear Pope, what are your memories of your First Communion day?

I would first like to say thank you for this celebration of faith that you are offering to me, for your presence and for your joy. I greet you and thank you for the hug I have received from some of you, a hug that, of course, symbolically stands for you all.

As for the question, of course I remember my First Communion day very well. It was a lovely Sunday in March 1936, sixty-nine years ago. It was a sunny day, the church looked very beautiful, there was music.... There were so many beautiful things that I remember. There were about thirty of us, boys and girls from my little village of no more than 500 inhabitants.

But at the heart of my joyful and beautiful memories is this one—and your spokesperson said the same thing: I understood that Jesus had entered my heart, he had actually visited me. And with Jesus, God himself was with me. And I realized that this is a gift of love that is truly worth more than all the other things that life can give.

So on that day I was really filled with great joy because Jesus came to me, and I realized that a new stage in my life was beginning—I was nine years old—and that it was henceforth important to stay faithful to that encounter, to that communion. I promised the Lord as best I could: "I want to stay with you always," and I prayed to him, "but above all, stay with me." So I went on living my life like that; thanks be to God, the Lord has always taken me by the hand and guided me, even in difficult situations.

Thus, that day of my First Communion was the beginning of a journey made together. I hope that for all of you, too, the First Communion you have received in this Year of the Eucharist will be the beginning of a lifelong friendship with Jesus, the beginning of a journey together, because in walking with Jesus we do well and life becomes good.

Livia: Holy Father, before the day of my First Communion I went to confession. I have also been to confession on other occasions. I wanted to ask you: Do I have to go to confession every time I receive Communion, even when I have committed the same sins? Because I realize that they are always the same.

I will tell you two things. The first, of course, is that you do not always have to go to confession before you receive Communion unless you have committed such serious sins that they need to be confessed. Therefore, it is not necessary to make one's confession before every Eucharistic Communion. This is the first point. It is only necessary when you have committed a really serious sin, when you have deeply offended Jesus, so that your friendship is destroyed and you have to start again. Only in that case, when you are in a state of "mortal" sin, in other words, grave sin, is it necessary to go to confession before Communion. This is my first point.

My second point: even if, as I said, it is not necessary to go to confession before each Communion, it is very helpful to confess with a certain regularity. It is true: our sins are always the same, but we clean our homes, our rooms, at least once a week, even if the dirt is always the same; in order to live in cleanliness, in order to start again. Otherwise, the dirt might not be seen, but it builds up. Something similar can be said about the soul, for me myself: if I never go to confession, my soul is neglected, and in the end I am always pleased with myself and no longer understand that I must always work hard to improve, that I must make progress. And this cleansing of the soul that Jesus gives us in the Sacrament of Confession helps us to make our consciences more alert, more open, and, hence, it also helps us to mature spiritually and as human persons. Therefore, two things: confession is only necessary in the case of a serious sin, but it is very helpful to confess regularly in order to foster cleanliness and beauty of the soul and to mature day by day in life.

Andrea: In preparing me for my First Communion day, my catechist told me that Jesus is present in the Eucharist. But how? I can't see him!

No, we cannot see him, but there are many things we do not see even though they exist and are essential. For example: We do not see our reason, yet we have reason. We do not see our intelligence, and we have it. In a word: we do not see our soul, and yet it exists and we see its effects, because we can speak, think, and make decisions, etc. Nor do we see an electric current, for example, yet we see that it exists; we see this microphone, that it is working, and we see lights. Therefore, we do not see the very deepest things, those that really sustain life and the world, but we can see and feel their effects. This is also true for electricity; we do not see the electric current, but we see the light.

So it is with the risen Lord: we do not see him with our eyes, but we see that wherever Jesus is, people change, they improve. A greater capacity for peace, for reconciliation, etc., is created. Therefore, we do not see the Lord himself, but we see the effects of the Lord: so we can understand that Jesus is present. And as I said, it is precisely the invisible things that are the most profound, the most important. So let us go to meet this invisible but powerful Lord who helps us to live well.

Giulia: Your Holiness, everyone tells us that it is important to go to Mass on Sunday. We would gladly go to it, but often our parents do not take us because on Sundays they sleep. The parents of a friend of mine work in a shop, and we often go to the country to visit our grandparents. Could you say something to them, to make them understand that it is important to go to Mass together on Sundays?

I would think so, of course, with great love and great respect for your parents, because they certainly have a lot to do. However, with a daughter's respect and love, you could say to them: "Dear Mommy, dear Daddy, it is so important for us all, even for you, to meet Jesus. This encounter enriches us. It is an important element in our lives. Let's find a little time together, we can find an opportunity. Perhaps there is also a possibility where Grandma lives." In brief, I would say, with great love and respect for your parents, I would tell them: "Please understand that this is not only important for me, it is not only catechists who say it, it is important for us all. And it will be the light of Sunday for all our family."

Alessandro: What good does it do for our everyday life to go to Holy Mass and receive Communion?

It centers life. We live amid so many things. And the people who do not go to church do not know that it is precisely

Jesus they lack. But they feel that something is missing in their lives. If God is absent from my life, if Jesus is absent from my life, a guide, an essential friend is missing, even an important joy for life, the strength to grow as a man, to overcome my vices and mature as a human being.

Therefore, we cannot immediately see the effects of being with Jesus and of going to Communion. But with the passing of the weeks and years, we feel more and more keenly the absence of God, the absence of Jesus. It is a fundamental and destructive incompleteness. I could easily speak of countries where atheism has prevailed for years: how souls are destroyed, but also the earth. In this way we can see that it is important, and I would say fundamental, to be nourished by Jesus in Communion. It is he who gives us enlightenment, offers us guidance for our lives, a guidance that we need.

Anna: Dear Pope, can you explain to us what Jesus meant when he said to the people who were following him: "I am the bread of life"?

First of all, perhaps we should explain clearly what bread is. Today, we have a refined cuisine, rich in very different foods, but in simpler situations bread is the basic source of nourishment; and when Jesus called himself the Bread of Life, the bread is, shall we say, the initial, an abbreviation that stands for all nourishment. And as we need to nourish our bodies in order to live, so we also need to nourish our spirits, our souls, and our wills. As human persons, we have not only bodies but also souls; we are thinking beings with minds and wills. We must also nourish our spirits and our souls, so that they can develop and truly attain their fulfillment. And therefore, if Jesus says: "I am the bread of life", it means that Jesus himself is the nourishment we need for our soul, for our inner self, because the soul also needs food. And technical things do not suffice, although they are so important. We really need God's friendship, which helps us to make the right decisions. We need to mature as human beings. In other words: Jesus nourishes us so that we can truly become mature people and our lives can become good.

Adriano: Holy Father, they told us that today we will have Eucharistic adoration. What is it? How is it done? Can you explain it to us? Thank you.

We will see straightaway what adoration is and how it is done, because everything has been properly prepared for it: we will say prayers, we will sing, kneel, and in this way we will be in Jesus' presence.

But of course, your question requires a deeper answer: not only how you do adoration but what adoration is. I would say: adoration is recognizing that Jesus is my Lord, that Jesus shows me the way to take, and that I will live well only if I know the road that Jesus points out and follow the path he shows me.

Therefore, adoration means saying: "Jesus, I am yours. I will follow you in my life. I never want to lose this friendship, this communion with you." I could also say that adoration is essentially an embrace with Jesus in which I say to him: "I am yours, and I ask you, please stay with me always."

IX

Entering into the Mystery of the Grain of Wheat

From a Homily at Saint Paul outside the Walls, Rome, October 16, 1993

You seek the living God. Life, however, can be given only by living. More has to happen, therefore, than mere talk. This is why Christ enters into the fate of the dying grain of wheat, so that the husk might break open and the mature fruit might emerge from the husk. This is why he enters into the mystery of the Cross, so that, when lifted up above and beyond the whole world, he might become visible to all and speak to all and give to everyone more than words: himself and, in himself, the life of the living God.

He enters into the Cross and Resurrection because only in that way does he become completely word and life. Through the Cross and Resurrection, he is no longer bound to this or that place, but is with everyone and gives

This translation is taken, with corrections, from Joseph Ratzinger, *Teaching and Learning the Love of God: Being a Priest Today*, ed. Pierluca Azzaro and Carlos Granados, trans. Michael J. Miller (San Francisco: Ignatius Press, 2017), 112–17. Published in German as "Eingehen in das Geheimnis des Weizenkorns", for the ordination of five candidates of the Integrierte Gemeinde in Saint Paul outside the Walls on October 16, 1993, in *30 Jahre Wegbegleitung: Joseph Ratzinger, Papst Benedikt XVI. und die Katholische Integrierte Gemeinde*, ed. Arnold Stötzel, Traudl Wallbrecher, and Ludwig Weimer (Bad Tölz, 2006), 82–85.

them more than talk, gives them the life of the living God. And this is the only way it can happen, in this surrender of his life; only in this way does the grain of wheat break open and the fruit develop down through all the ages of history. The Gospel of John continues with a series of sayings about "keeping and losing life" in which the Lord then extends this teaching to his disciples. They will go out and bring him, the Crucified and Risen One, to the people, as we can experience it so awesomely and dramatically here in this place where Paul, the Apostle to the Gentiles, gave his life with Christ and for Christ and, thus, with him for the world. They, too, cannot come with mere talk. They can bring him only by laying their life down in his, by surrendering themselves with him to the law of the dying grain of wheat, and, thus, through their own life bringing the living Word himself.

Because this is so, the messenger of Jesus Christ can therefore never be merely a public speaker or a specialist proposing a particular theory. Therefore the ministry of the messenger is a sacramental ministry, which means a ministry in which word and being belong to each other. And here, again, this cannot take the form of him giving himself in a heroic deed—what difference would he make?—but, rather, he must allow himself to be taken by the Lord, to die into him; in this way the Lord comes through him to the people. We call this sacrament, the fact that beyond all his own activity, beyond all his own ability and knowledge, this mystery of death occurs, this transfer of ownership to him, being accepted by him, so that he speaks, lives, and is present through us. In the rite of priestly ordination, which we are experiencing right now, this is depicted in a very vivid way especially in the ceremony of robing the candidate in liturgical vestments. The candidate is robed, a passive verb; I myself cannot take the vestments as my own, as we heard in the Second Reading. No one takes the priesthood upon himself. Indeed, that would just be his own act, and in the end he would remain merely what he has to give with his sorry ego. I must be robed. I must be taken by him, so that he may be there through me. Thus this ceremony of being robed signifies precisely the immersion of my ego in him. "Take me away from myself and give me to you as your own"—I leave myself to you, so that you might act and work through me and be among the people. Of course, all this—this self-abandonment, this allowing the ego to be immersed and to disappear in him, and so too this placing of my own will in his—very profoundly contradicts our attitude toward life, and I suppose this has been the case in every age. For, indeed, this ego is precisely what we want to assert; we want to fulfill it, put ourselves forward, have ownership of our life, and thereby draw the world into ourselves and enjoy it and leave a trace of ourselves in such a way that this ego persists and keeps its importance in the world.

It is characteristic of the present era that the so-called single life is on the increase and an ever greater, ever more dominant sector of the population is made up of persons who enter no lasting relationship but are just "I" and lead only this life of their own. And, indeed, there is something like an almost traumatic fear of fruitfulness, because the other might take our place away, because we feel that our share of existence is threatened. And ultimately this retreat into wanting to be only myself is fear of death, fear of losing life, all that we have and are.

But as the Lord tells us in the Gospel: Precisely this desperate attempt to possess the ego entirely after all, to possess at least this and as much of the world as can possibly fit into this ego, leads to it becoming withered and empty. For man, who is created in the image of the triune God, cannot find himself by closing himself up in himself. He can find himself only in relation, in going out, in self-giving, in the gesture of the dying grain of wheat.

Becoming a priest means that we accept in a very specific way this call of the Lord from today's Gospel, that we say yes: Lord, take me as I am, make me as you want me to be; I give myself into your hands, I make myself over to you. The Gospel concludes with the saying: "If anyone wants to be my servant, he will be where I am, and the Father will honor him." Being a priest means becoming *diakonos Christou*, the servant of Christ; and this means not being at my own place, at the place sought out by my ego for itself, but rather: being where he is.

I think that this is actually the quintessential description of priestly ministry: Being where he is, seeking him, being at his disposal, belonging to him, walking with him, living with him, and this means again and again being in the mystery of the Cross and Resurrection. For this is his permanent place, the place of his suffering in the world and at the same time the place of his glory, because right from this allowing-oneself-to-break-open proceeds the divine mystery of fruitfulness and the shining forth of God's life into this world.

Then comes this wonderful promise: "The Father will honor him." We do not look for honor from men; we are not status seekers. For then we have to bow also to people's opinions, submit to public opinion, which is considered an instrument of freedom but in truth is genuine slavery that lifts people up and drops them again.... That is not what we seek. The truth will make you free and enable you to get out of the endless search for opinions. We look to the truth of God, to the mystery of Jesus Christ, and by being with him we are certainly at the place of insignificance, at the place of the Cross in this world, but precisely thereby in God's glory, in the light of his face upon this world. If we seek God's honor, seek the truth, we stand in his honor. And this is authentic salvation, freedom, and life, not only for us but for others.

X

Filled with the Lord's Joy

Meeting with Priests at the Prayer Vigil,
International Meeting of Priests,
June 10, 2010

*Holy Father, I am Don José Eduardo Oliveira y Silva, and I come
from America, namely Brazil. Most of us here are committed to the
parish apostolate, and not to just one community. Sometimes we
pastors are in charge of several parishes or else of particularly large
communities. We try our best to meet the needs of a society that
has changed much; it is no longer entirely Christian, and we come
to realize that our "doing" is not enough. How should we proceed,
Your Holiness? What direction should we take?*

Dear friends, first of all I would like to express my great
joy because gathered here are priests from all parts of the
world, in the joy of our vocation and in our willingness to
serve with all our strength the Lord in our time. In regard
to the question, I am well aware that today it is very difficult to be a parish priest, also and above all in the countries
of ancient Christianity. Parishes have become more exten-
sive pastoral units ... and it is impossible to know everyone; it is impossible to do all the work we would expect
of a parish priest. So really, we are wondering how to
proceed, as you said. But I would first like to say: I know
there are many parish priests in the world who really give

all their strength for evangelization, for the Lord's presence, and for his sacraments. And to these faithful parish priests who work with all the strength of their lives, with our being passionate for Christ, I want to say a big "thank you" at this moment. I said that it is not possible to do all we would like to do, that perhaps we should do, because our strength is limited, and there are difficult situations in an increasingly diversified, more complicated society. I think that, above all, it is important that the faithful be able to see that the priest does not just perform a "job" with working hours, and then is free and lives only for himself, but that he is a passionate man of Christ who carries in himself the fire of Christ's love. If the faithful see that he is full of the joy of the Lord and understand also that he cannot do everything, they can accept limits and help the parish priest. This seems to me the most important point: that we can see and feel that the parish priest really feels his call from the Lord, that he is full of love for the Lord and for his faithful. If there is this, you understand and you can also see the impossibility of doing everything. So, being full of the joy of the Gospel with our whole being is the first condition. Then they must make choices, have priorities, to see what is possible and what is impossible. I would say that we know the three fundamental priorities: they are the three pillars of our being priests. First, the Eucharist, the sacraments. The Eucharist: to make possible and present the Eucharist, above all on Sundays, for as many as possible, for everyone, and to celebrate it so that it becomes really the visible act of the Lord's love for us. Then, the Proclamation of the Word in all its dimensions: from the personal dialogue to the homily. The third point is *caritas*, the love of Christ: to be present for the suffering, for the little ones, for the children, for people in difficulty, for the marginalized; to make really present the love

of the Good Shepherd. And then, a very high priority is
also the personal relationship with Christ. In the breviary,
on November 4, we read a beautiful text by Saint Charles
Borromeo, a great shepherd, who truly gave all of himself
and says to us, to all priests, "Do not neglect your own
soul. If your soul is neglected, even to others you cannot
give what you should give. Thus, even for yourself, for
your soul, you must have time." Or, in other words, the
personal colloquy with Christ, the personal dialogue with
Christ, is a fundamental pastoral priority in our work for
the others! And prayer is not a marginal thing: it is the
"occupation" of the priest to pray, as representative of
the people who do not know how to pray or do not find
time to pray. The personal prayer, especially the Liturgy
of the Hours, is fundamental nourishment for our soul,
for all our actions. Finally, to recognize our limitations,
to open ourselves up even to this humility. Recall a scene
from Mark, chapter 6, where the disciples are "stressed
out"; they want to do everything, and the Lord says:
"Come away by yourselves to a lonely place, and rest a
while" (Mk 6:31). Even this is work, I would say, pastoral
work: to find and to have the humility, the courage to rest.
So, I think, that passion for the Lord, love for the Lord,
shows us the priorities, the choices, helps us to find the
road. The Lord will help us. Thank you all!

*Your Holiness, . . . you are a pope-theologian, while we, when
we can, just read some books on theology for formation. However,
it seems to us that a rift has been created between theology and
doctrine, and even more between theology and spirituality. One
feels the need for studies that are not all academic but nourish our
spirituality. We feel the need in the same pastoral ministry. At
times theology does not seem to have God and Jesus Christ at the
center as the first "theological place", but it instead has diffused*

tastes and trends. The consequence is the proliferation of subjective opinions permitting the introduction, even in the Church, of non-Catholic thought. How can we stay focused in our lives and in our ministry, when it is the world judging faith and not vice versa? We feel "off-center"!

Thank you. You touched upon a very difficult and painful problem. There is actually a theology that wants above all to be academic, to appear scientific, and forgets the vital reality, the presence of God, his presence among us, his talking today not just in the past. Even Saint Bonaventure distinguished two forms of theology in his time and said: "There is a theology that comes from the arrogance of reason, that wants to dominate everything; God passes from being the subject to the object of our study, while he should be the subject who speaks and guides us." There is really this abuse of theology, which is the arrogance of reason and does not nurture faith but overshadows God's presence in the world. Then, there is a theology that wants to know more out of love for the beloved; it is stirred by love and guided by love. It wants to know the beloved more. And this is the true theology that comes from love of God, of Christ, and it wants to enter more deeply into communion with Christ. In reality, temptations today are great. Above all, it imposes the so-called "modern vision of the world" (Bultmann, *modernes Weltbild*), which becomes the criterion of what would be possible or impossible. And so, because of this very criterion that everything is as usual, that all historical events are of the same type, the newness of the Gospel is excluded, the irruption of God is excluded, the real news that is the joy of our faith. What should we do? I would say first to all theologians: Have courage. And I would like to say a big "thank you" to the many theologians who do a good job. There are abuses, we know, but in all parts of the world there are many theologians who truly live the Word of God. They are nourished by meditation, are living the faith of the Church, and want to help so that faith is present in our today. To these theologians I would like to say a big "thank you". And I would say to theologians in general: Do not be afraid of this phantom of science! I have been following theology since 1946. I began to study theology in January '46, and, therefore, I have seen about three generations of theologians, and I can say that the hypotheses that in that time, and then in the 1960s and 1980s, were the newest, absolutely scientific, absolutely *almost* dogmatic, have since aged and are no longer valid! Many of them seem almost ridiculous. So, have the courage to resist the apparently scientific approach, do not submit to all the hypotheses of the moment, but really start thinking from the great faith of the Church, which is present in all times and opens for us access to the truth. Above all, do not think that positivistic thinking, which excludes the transcendent that is inaccessible, is true reason! This weak reasoning, which only considers things that can be experienced, is really an insufficient reasoning. We theologians must use a broader reason that is open to the greatness of God. We must have the courage to go beyond positivism to the question about the roots of being. This seems to me of great importance. Therefore, we must have the courage to use the great, broader reason, and we must have the humility not to submit to all the hypotheses of the moment and to live by the great faith of the Church of all times. There is no majority against the majority of the saints. Saints are the true majority in the Church, and we must orient ourselves by the saints! Then, to the seminarians and priests I say the same. Do not think that Sacred Scripture is an isolated book; it is living in the living community of the

Church, which is the same subject in all ages and guarantees the presence of the Word of God. The Lord has given us the Church as a live subject with the structure of the bishops in communion with the pope. This great reality of the bishops of the world in communion with the pope guarantees to us the testimony of permanent truth. We trust this permanent Magisterium of the communion of the bishops with the pope, which represents to us the presence of the Word. Besides, we also trust in the life of the Church while, above all, exercising critical thought. Certainly theological formation—I would like to tell seminarians—is very important. In our time, we must know Sacred Scripture well, in order to combat the attacks of the sects. We must really be friends of the Word. We must also know the currents of our time to respond reasonably in order to give—as Saint Peter says—"reason for our faith". Formation is very important. But we must also be critical. The criterion of faith is the criterion with which to see also theologians and theologies. Pope John Paul II gave us an absolutely sure criterion in the *Catechism of the Catholic Church*. Here we see the synthesis of our faith, and this catechism is truly the criterion by which we can judge whether a given theology is acceptable or not. So, I recommend the reading, the study, of this text, so we can go forward with a critical theology in the positive sense. That is critical of the trends of fashion and open to the true news, the inexhaustible depths of the Word of God, which reveals itself anew in all times, even in our time.

Holy Father, ... when I am celebrating Mass, I find myself, and I understand that there I meet my identity as well as the root and energy of my ministry. The Sacrifice of the Cross reveals to me the Good Shepherd who gives all of himself for the flock, for each sheep. And when I say: "This is my body ... this is my

blood" given and poured out as a sacrifice for you, then I under-
stand the beauty of celibacy and obedience, which I promised freely
at the moment of my ordination. Despite the natural difficulties,
celibacy seems obvious to me, looking at Christ. But I am stunned
to read so much worldly criticism of this gift. I ask humbly, Holy
Father, to enlighten us about the depth and the true meaning of
ecclesiastical celibacy.

Thank you for the two parts of your question. The first, which shows the permanent and vital foundation of our celibacy. The second, which shows all the difficulties in which we find ourselves in our times. The first part is important, i.e., the center of our life must really be the daily celebration of the Holy Eucharist. Central here are the words of Consecration: "This is my Body, this is my Blood", which means that we speak "in persona Christi". Christ allows us to use his "I", we speak in the "I" of Christ. Christ is "drawing us into himself" and allows us to be united. He unites us to his "I". So, through this action, the fact that he "draws" us to himself so that our "I" becomes united to his, he realizes the permanence, the uniqueness of his Priesthood. Therefore, he is at all times the unique Priest. Yet, he is very present to the world because he "draws" us to himself and so renders present his priestly mission. This means that we are "drawn" to the God of Christ. It is this union with his "I" that is realized in the words of the Consecration. Also in the "I absolve you", because none of us could absolve from sins, it is the "I" of Christ, of God, who alone can absolve. This unification of his "I" with ours implies that we are "drawn" also into the reality of his Resurrection; we are going forth toward the full life of resurrection. Jesus speaks of it to the Sadducees in Matthew 22. It is a "new" life in which we are already beyond marriage (cf. Mt 22:23–32). It is important that we always allow this identification of the "I" of Christ with us, this being "drawn" toward the world of resurrection. In this sense, celibacy is anticipation. We transcend this time and move on. By doing so, we "draw" ourselves and our time toward the world of the resurrection, toward the newness of Christ, toward a new and true life. Therefore, celibacy is an anticipation, a foretaste, made possible by the grace of the Lord, who draws us to himself, toward the world of the resurrection. It invites us always anew to transcend ourselves and the present time, to the true presence of the future that becomes present today. And here we come to a very important point. One great problem of Christianity in today's world is that it does not think anymore of the future of God. The present of this world alone seems sufficient. We want to have only this world, to live only in this world. So we close the doors to the true greatness of our existence. The meaning of celibacy as an anticipation of the future is to open these doors, to make the world greater, to show the reality of the future that should be lived by us already as present. Living, then, as a testimony of faith: we truly believe that God exists, that God enters into my life, and that I can found my life on Christ, on the future life. And now we know the worldly criticism of which you spoke. It is true that for the agnostic world, the world in which God does not enter, celibacy is a great scandal, because it shows exactly that God is considered and experienced as reality. With the eschatological dimension of celibacy, the future world of God enters into the reality of our time. And should this disappear!?

In a certain sense, this continuous criticism against celibacy may surprise in a time when it is becoming increasingly fashionable not to get married. But this not-getting-married is something totally, fundamentally different from celibacy. The avoidance of marriage is based on a will to live only for oneself, of not accepting any definitive tie, to have the life of every moment in full autonomy, to decide at any time what to do, what to take from life; and therefore a "no" to the bond, a "no" to definitiveness, to have life for oneself alone. While celibacy is just the opposite: it is a definitive "yes". It is to let oneself be taken in the hand of God, to give oneself into the hands of the Lord, into his "I". And therefore, it is an act of loyalty and trust, an act that also implies the fidelity of marriage. It is the opposite of this "no", of this autonomy that accepts no obligations, which will not enter into a bond. It is the definitive "yes" that supposes, confirms the definitive "yes" of marriage. And this marriage is the biblical form, a natural way of being man and woman, the foundation of the great Christian culture, of great cultures around the world. And if that disappears, the root of our culture will be destroyed. So celibacy confirms the "yes" of marriage with its "yes" to the future world. So, we want to go ahead and make present this scandal of a faith that bases all existence on God. We know that besides this great scandal that the world does not want to recognize, there are also the secondary scandals of our shortcomings, our sins, which obscure the true and great scandal and make people think: "They are not really living on the foundation of God." But there is also so much loyalty! Celibacy—as its adverse criticism shows—is a great sign of faith, of the presence of God in the world. We pray to the Lord to help us, to set us free from the secondary scandals in order to make relevant the great scandal of our faith: the confidence, the strength of our life, which is founded in God and in Jesus Christ!

Holy Father, . . . the priestly model that Your Holiness has given us this year, the Curé of Ars, sees at the center of our life and ministry the Eucharist, the Sacrament of Penance, and personal repentance; and love for worship, worthily celebrated. I see before me signs of the rigorous poverty of Saint John Vianney and his passion for everything connected to worship. How can we live these fundamental aspects of our priestly life without falling into clericalism or an estrangement from reality that the world today does not permit us?

Thank you. So the question is how to live the centrality of the Eucharist without conducting a purely cultic life, as a stranger to the everyday life of other people. We know that clericalism is a temptation for priests in all ages, today as well. And it is even more important to find the true way to live the Eucharist, which is not closure to the world, but openness to the world's needs. We must keep in mind that in the Eucharist is realized this great drama of God who goes out of himself, leaves, as said in the Letter to the Philippians, his own glory, goes out and lowers himself to be one of us, even unto death on the Cross (cf. Phil 2). This is the adventure of God's love, which leaves, abandons himself to be with us—and this becomes present in the Eucharist. The great act, the great adventure of God's love is the humility of God who gives himself to us. In this sense, the Eucharist is to be considered as entering into this path of God. Saint Augustine says in *De Civitate Dei*, book 10: "Hoc est sacrificium Christianorum: multi unum corpus in Christo", i.e., the sacrifice of Christians is being united by love of Christ in the unity of the one Body of Christ. The sacrifice consists precisely in going out of ourselves, in allowing entrance into the communion of the one bread, of the one Body, and, therefore, to enter into the great adventure of God's love. So, we must celebrate, live, and meditate always on the Eucharist, as the school of liberation from my "I": to enter into the one bread, which is the Bread of all that unites us in the one Body of Christ. Therefore, the Eucharist is, in itself, an act of love, and it obliges us to this reality of love for others: that the sacrifice of Christ is the communion of all in his Body. So, this is how we must learn the Eucharist, which then is the opposite of clericalism, of closure in oneself. We think also of Mother Teresa, truly the great example in this century, at this time. A love that leaves itself, which leaves every type of clericalism, of estrangement from the world, and goes to the most marginalized, to the poorest, to those nearing death, and totally gives herself up to love of the poor, the marginalized. But Mother Teresa, who gave us this example and the community that follows in her steps, supposed always as the first condition of one foundation the presence of a tabernacle. Without the presence of the love of God who gives himself, it would not have been possible to realize that apostolate. It would not have been possible to live in that abandonment to self. They could and can perform today this great act of love, this openness to all, only by inserting their self-abandonment in God, in this adventure of God, this humility of God. In this sense, I would say that living the Eucharist in its original sense, in its true depth, is a school of life. It is the surest protection against the temptation of clericalism.

Most Holy Father, ... here tonight are many priests. But we know that our seminaries are not full and that in the future, in various parts of the world, we expect a decline, even a sharp one. What can we do to encourage new vocations? How can we propose our way of living, all that is great and beautiful in it, to a young man of our time?

Thank you. You, too, have touched upon a great and painful problem of our time: the lack of vocations, because of which local churches are in danger of perishing, for lack of the Word of life, missing the presence of the Eucharist and other sacraments. What's to be done? The temptation to take things into our own hands is great, the temptation to transform the priesthood—the Sacrament of Christ, the fact of being chosen by him—into a normal profession, a "job" with specific working hours, and for the rest one belongs only to oneself. If we do so, we make it just like any other vocation; we make it accessible and easy. But this is a temptation that does not solve the problem. It reminds me of the story of Saul, the King of Israel, who before the battle against the Philistines waits for Samuel for the necessary sacrifice to God. When Samuel does not arrive at the expected time, Saul himself makes the sacrifice, although not a priest (cf. 1 Sam 13). He thought to resolve the problem, which of course he does not, because if one tries to take in hand what he cannot do, if he makes himself God, or nearly so, then one cannot expect things really to go in the way of God. If we, too, only perform a profession like any other, giving up the sacred, the novelty, the diversity of the sacrament that only God can give, that can only come from his calling and not from our "doing", we would not solve anything. [We should all the more]—as the Lord invites us—pray to God, knock on his door, at the heart of God, to give us vocations; [we should] pray with great insistence, with great determination, even with great conviction. For God does not close himself to a persistent, permanent, confident prayer, even when he makes us wait, like Saul, beyond the time we expected. This seems to me the first point: to encourage the faithful to have this humility, this confidence, this courage to pray insistently for vocations, to knock at the heart of God to give us priests. In addition to this, I would like to make three points. The first: each of us should strive to live his priesthood in such a way as to be convincing. In such a manner that young people might say this is a true calling, one can live in this way, in this way one can do something essential for the world. I think that none of us would have become a priest if we had not met convincing priests who were on fire with the love of Christ. So this is the first point: Let us strive to be convincing priests. The second point is that we must invite, as I said before, people to join in prayer, to have this humility, this trust to speak to God forcefully, decisively. The third point: have the courage to talk with young people about whether God is calling them, because often a human word is required to open one to hear the divine call. Talk with young people and especially help them find a vital context in which they can live. Today's world is such that the maturation of a priestly vocation seems to be ruled out. Young people need environments in which to live their faith, in which to experience the beauty of faith, in which to feel that this is a way of life, "the" way of life. And help them find movements, [or a parish—the community within a parish—or other settings] where they really are surrounded by faith, by God's love, and can therefore become open so that the call of God may arrive and help them. Moreover, we thank the Lord for all the seminarians of our time, for the young priests, and we pray. The Lord will help us! Thank you all!

XI

An Oasis in Which to
Draw Living Water

Homily for the Carthusian Monks
of Serra San Bruno, October 9, 2011

I thank the Lord who has brought me to this place of
faith and prayer, the Charterhouse of Serra San Bruno....
Today I come to you ..., and I would like our meeting
to highlight the deep bond that exists between Peter and
Bruno, between pastoral service to the Church's unity
and the contemplative vocation in the Church. Ecclesial
communion, in fact, demands an inner force, that force
which Father Prior has just recalled, citing the expression "captus ab Uno", ascribed to Saint Bruno: "grasped
by the One", by God, "Unus potens per omnia" (the
Almighty One present throughout creation), as we sang
in the Vespers hymn. From the contemplative community the ministry of pastors draws a spiritual sap that
comes from God.

"Fugitiva relinquere et aeterna captare": to abandon
transient realities and seek to grasp that which is eternal.
These words from the letter your founder addressed to
Ralph, provost of Rheims, contain the core of your spirituality (cf. *Epistola ad Radulphum*, no. 13): the strong desire
to enter into union of life with God, abandoning everything

else, everything that stands in the way of this communion, and letting oneself be grasped by the immense love of God to live this love alone.

Dear brothers, you have found the hidden treasure, the pearl of great value (cf. Mt 13:44–46); you have responded radically to Jesus' invitation: "If you would be perfect, go, sell what you possess and give to the poor, and you will have treasure in heaven; and come, follow me" (Mt 19:21). Every monastery—male or female—is an oasis in which the deep well, from which to draw "living water" to quench our deepest thirst, is constantly being dug with prayer and meditation. However, the Charterhouse is a special oasis in which silence and solitude are preserved with special care, in accordance with the form of life founded by Saint Bruno that has remained unchanged down the centuries. "I live in a rather faraway hermitage ... with some religious brothers" is the concise sentence that your founder wrote (*Epistola ad Radulphum*, no. 4). The Successor of Peter's visit to this historic Charterhouse is intended to strengthen not only those of you who live here but the entire Order in its mission, which is more than ever timely and meaningful in today's world.

Technical progress, especially in the area of transport and communications, has made human life more comfortable but also more keyed up, at times even frenetic. Cities are almost always noisy; silence is rarely to be found in them because there is always background noise, in some areas even at night. In recent decades, moreover, the development of the media has spread and extended a phenomenon that had already been outlined in the 1960s: virtuality risks predominating over reality. Unbeknownst to them, people are increasingly becoming immersed in a virtual dimension because of the audiovisual messages that accompany their life from morning to night.

The youngest, born into this condition, seem to want to fill every empty moment with music and images, out of fear of feeling this very emptiness. This is a trend that has always existed, especially among the young and in the more developed urban contexts, but today it has reached a level such as to give rise to talk about anthropological mutation. Some people are no longer able to remain for long periods in silence and solitude.

I chose to mention this sociocultural condition because it highlights the specific charism of the Charterhouse as a precious gift for the Church and for the world, a gift that contains a deep message for our life and for the whole of humanity. I shall sum it up like this: by withdrawing into silence and solitude, human beings, so to speak, "expose" themselves to reality in their nakedness, to that apparent "void", which I mentioned at the outset, in order to experience instead Fullness, the presence of God, of the most real Reality that exists and that lies beyond the tangible dimension. He is a perceptible presence in every creature: in the air that we breathe, in the light that we see and that warms us, in the grass, in stones.... God, *Creator omnium* (the Creator of all), passes through all things but is beyond them and for this very reason is the foundation of them all.

The monk, in leaving everything, "takes a risk", as it were: he exposes himself to solitude and silence in order to live on nothing but the essential, and precisely in living on the essential he also finds a deep communion with his brethren, with every human being.

Some might think that it would suffice to come here to take this "leap". But it is not like this. This vocation, like every vocation, finds an answer in an ongoing process, in a life-long search. Indeed it is not enough to withdraw to a place such as this in order to learn to be in God's presence. Just as in marriage it is not enough to celebrate the sacrament to become effectively one, but it is necessary to let God's grace act and to walk together through the daily routine of conjugal life, so becoming monks requires time, practice, and patience. "In a divine and persevering vigilance", as Saint Bruno said, they "await the return of their Lord so that they might be able to open the door to him as soon as he knocks" (*Epistola ad Radulphum*, no. 4); and the beauty of every vocation in the Church consists precisely in this: giving God time to act with his Spirit and to one's own humanity to form itself, to grow in that particular state of life according to the measure of the maturity of Christ.

In Christ there is everything, fullness; we need time to make one of the dimensions of his mystery our own. We could say that this is a journey of transformation in which the mystery of Christ's Resurrection is brought about and made manifest in us, a mystery of which the Word of God in the biblical reading from the Letter to the Romans has reminded us this evening: the Holy Spirit who raised Jesus from the dead and will give life to our mortal bodies (cf. Rom 8:11) is the One who also brings about our configuration to Christ in accordance with each one's vocation, a journey that unwinds from the baptismal font to death, a passing on to the Father's house. In the world's eyes, it sometimes seems impossible to spend one's whole life in a monastery, but in fact a whole life barely suffices to enter into this union with God, into this essential and profound Reality that is Jesus Christ.

This is why I have come here, dear Brothers who make up the Carthusian Community of Serra San Bruno, to tell you that the Church needs you and that you need the Church! Your place is not on the fringes: no vocation in the People of God is on the fringes. We are one body, in which every member is important and has the same dignity and is inseparable from the whole. You too, who live in voluntary isolation, are in the heart of the Church and make the pure blood of contemplation and of the love of God course through her veins.

Stat Crux dum volvitur orbis (the Cross is steady while the world is turning), your motto says. The Cross of Christ is the firm point in the midst of the world's changes and upheavals. Life in a charterhouse shares in the stability of the Cross, which is that of God, of God's faithful love. By remaining firmly united to Christ, like the branches to the Vine, may you, too, dear Carthusian Brothers, be associated with his mystery of salvation, like the Virgin Mary who *stabat* (stood) beneath the Cross, united with her Son in the same sacrifice of love.

Thus, like Mary and with her, you too are deeply inserted in the mystery of the Church, a sacrament of union of men with God and with each other. In this you are singularly close to my ministry.

May the Most Holy Mother of the Church therefore watch over us and the holy Father Bruno always bless your community from Heaven. Amen.

XII

The Grandeur of Man Is His
Resemblance to God

Speech at the International Conference
of the Pontifical Council for
Health Care Workers, November 28, 1996

The subject of this international conference brings disturbing memories to my mind. Please allow me, by way of
introduction, to give you an account of my own personal
experience. We return here to 1941, and thus to wartime
and to the National Socialist regime. One of our aunts
whom we visited very often was the mother of a strong and
healthy child who was a few years younger than myself.
However, he increasingly displayed the symptoms of the
Down syndrome. The simplicity of his clouded mind
aroused affection, and his mother, who had already lost
a child who died early on in life, was bound to him by
sincere ties. But in 1941 the authorities of the Third Reich
ordered him to be taken to an institution to receive better
care and assistance. At that time it was not yet suspected
that an elimination of the mentally handicapped was being
carried out, even though this program had already been

Joseph Cardinal Ratzinger, "The Likeness of God in the Human Being",
Dolentium Hominum 34, no. 1 (1997): 16–19. Translation modified for style by
Ignatius Press.

set in motion. After a little while the news arrived that the child had died of pneumonia and that his body had been cremated. From that moment on, news of this kind became ever more frequent.

In the village where we had previously lived, we used to most readily visit a widow who did not have any children and who was very happy if the children in the neighborhood went to see her. The little piece of land that her father had left her barely provided her with a livelihood. She was in good spirits even though she was rather afraid about the future. Later we learned that the loneliness which afflicted her more and more had increasingly darkened her mind. Her worries about the future had become pathological because she was always anxious about what the future would bring—perhaps she would no longer have food to put in her mouth. She was then identified as mentally disturbed and placed in an institution, and in this case as well, the news arrived that she had died from pneumonia.

A little later, exactly the same thing happened in our village. The small piece of property that was next to our house had previously been cultivated by three unmarried brothers to whom it belonged. It was alleged that they were mentally ill even though in actual fact they were able to look after their house and their property. They also disappeared into an institution, and soon afterward it was made known that they had died. At this point there could no longer be any doubt about what was happening—a systematic elimination of all those who were not considered productive. The state had arrogated to itself the right to decide who deserved to live and who was to be deprived of the right to exist on the grounds of advantage to the community or to the state, employing as a criterion the idea that an individual could be eliminated because he was not useful to others or to himself.

This fact added a new and different kind of anxiety to the horrors of war, which were themselves becoming ever more deeply felt: we were touched by the icy coldness of a logic based upon criteria of utility and power. We felt that the killing of these people humiliated and threatened us, the human essence that was within us. If patience and love dedicated to the suffering are eliminated from human existence because they are seen as a waste of time and money, not only do we do wrong to those who are killed, but those who survive are themselves mutilated in their spirits. We realized that when the mystery of God, his inviolable dignity, which is present in each and every man, is not respected, then not only are individuals threatened, but humanity itself is endangered. In the paralyzing silence, in the fear that held everyone in its grip, Cardinal Von Galen's condemnation was like a liberation—he broke the paralysis of that fear in order to defend man himself, the image of God, within the mentally disabled.

The luminous Word of God with which Genesis begins the account of the creation of man combats all threats to man caused by calculations about power and usefulness: "Let us make man in our image, after our likeness"—"faciamus hominem ad imaginem et similitudinem nostrum," in the words of the Vulgate (Gen 1:26). But what does this phrase mean? What is the divine likeness present in man? The term, as used by the Old Testament, is, so to speak, a monolith—it does not appear again in the Jewish Old Testament, even though Psalm 8 demonstrates an inner connection with it: "What is man that you are mindful of him?" (v. 4). The term is used again only in the sapiential writings. Sirach (17:2) roots the greatness of the human being in this fact without seeking to give an interpretation of what is actually meant by this likeness to God.

The Book of Wisdom (2:23) takes a further step forward and sees the state of being in the image of God as based in essential terms upon the immortality of man—what makes God God and distinguishes him from created man is precisely his immortality and everlastingness. Created man is in the image of God precisely because he participates in immortality—not because of his own nature, but as a result of a gift bestowed upon him by the Creator. The orientation toward eternal life is what makes man the created counterpart of God. This line of argument could be developed, and one could also say that eternal life means something more than mere eternal subsistence. It is full of meaning, and only in this way is it worthy of life and capable of eternity.

An orientation toward eternity, therefore, is an orientation toward the eternal communion of love with God, and the image of God thus bears the marks of its nature beyond earthly life. It cannot be determined in a static fashion and bound to some particular quality, but is a prosthesis of time beyond earthly life. It can be understood only with reference to its tension regarding the future, in its dynamic impulse toward eternity. Those who deny the existence of eternity and who see man as a merely terrestrial creature do not have any possibility—from the very outset—of penetrating the essence of the likeness of God. But this is only touched upon in the Book of Wisdom and fails to be developed further.

In this way the Old Testament leaves us with an unanswered question. We must recognize that Epiphanius was right when he declared—with reference to the various attempts to give a precise definition of the nature of this divine likeness—that we should not "seek to define the framework of the image but recognize its existence within man—if, that is, we do not want to abuse the grace of God"

(*Panarion*, LXX, 2, 7). But in truth we Christians always read the Old Testament within the context of the entire Bible, in its unity with the New Testament. From it we receive the key by which to achieve a sound and accurate reading of its texts. Just as the creation account of "In the beginning God created" receives its correct interpretation only in its rereading in the "In the beginning was the Word" of John's Gospel, so the same process is at work here.

Naturally enough, in this brief introductory talk, I cannot dwell at length upon the rich and multifaceted treatment of the subject that is to be found in the New Testament. I will confine myself to exploring two aspects of the question. It should be observed first and foremost—and this is a most important fact—that in the New Testament Christ is described as being "the image of God" (cf. 2 Cor 4:4; Col 1:15).

The Fathers of the Church made a linguistic observation here that cannot, perhaps, be really sustained, but that still certainly corresponds to the inner direction of the New Testament and its reinterpretation of the Old Testament. They declare that only Christ should be taught to be "the image of God". Man, on the other hand, is not the image but *ad imaginem*, created *in* the image, according to the image. He becomes an image of God in proportion to the degree to which he enters into communion with Christ and conforms to him. To put it in other words: the original image of man, which in turn represents the image of God, is Christ, and man is created by starting from his image, with reference to his image. The human creature is, at the same time as being such a creature, also a preliminary project in anticipation of Christ—or, rather, Christ is the fundamental idea of the Creator, and he forms man with a view to Christ, starting from this fundamental idea.

The ontological and spiritual dynamism that is hidden in this conception of things becomes especially evident in Romans 8:29 and 1 Corinthians 15:49, but it is also to be found in 2 Corinthians 4:6. According to Romans 8:29, men are predestined "to be conformed to the image of his Son, in order that he might be the first-born among many brethren". This conformity to the image of Christ is fulfilled in the Resurrection, by which he preceded us. Yet the Resurrection—and this should be made clear at this point—presupposes the Cross. The First Letter to the Corinthians makes a distinction between the first Adam, who became a "living soul" (15:45; cf Gen 2:7), and the last Adam, who became a Spirit giving life—"Just as we have borne the image of the man of dust, we shall also bear the image of the man of heaven" (15:49). Here we encounter a completely clear expression of the inner tension within the human being between clay and spirit, earth and Heaven, terrestrial origins and divine future.

This tension within the human being in time and beyond time belongs to the essence of man. And this tension determines what he is exactly at the center of life in this time. He is always on a journey toward himself or going away from himself; he is on a journey toward Christ or going away from him. He draws near to his original image, or he hides it and ruins it. The Innsbruck theologian F. Lakner has given fine expression to this dynamic conception of the divine likeness of man that is characteristic of the New Testament in the following way: "Man's being in the image of God is based upon predestination to divine filiation through mystical incorporation into Christ." Being an image is thus an inherent finality of man from the point of creation "towards God through participation in divine life in Christ".

However, we thus come to the decisive question of the subject here under discussion: Can this divine likeness be destroyed? And if it can, by what means? Are there human beings who are not in the image of God? In its radicalization of the doctrine of original sin, the Reformation gave an affirmative answer to this question and declared: Yes, through sin man can destroy the image of God within him and in fact has destroyed it. Indeed, man the sinner—who does not want to recognize God and does not respect man, or even kills him—does not represent the image of God, but deforms it, contradicts him who is Holiness, Truth, and Goodness. Bearing in mind what was said at the outset, this can and must bring us to the question: In whom is the image of God more obscured, more disfigured, or more extinguished—in the cold-blooded killer who is well aware of what he is doing, strong and perhaps intelligent as well, who makes himself God and derides God, or in the suffering innocent person in whom the light of reason glimmers weakly or is perhaps no longer discernible?

But such a question at this point is premature. First of all, a key point must be made—the radical thesis of the Reformation has been shown to be untenable, precisely when the Bible is taken as a point of departure. Man is in the image of God because he is man. And as long as he is man, a human being, he is mysteriously directed toward Christ, to the Son of God made man—and, therefore, oriented toward the mystery of God. The divine image is bound up with the human essence as such, and it is not within man's power to destroy that image completely.

But what man can certainly do is to disfigure the image, to achieve an inner contradiction with it. At this point, Lakner should be cited once again: "The divine force shines again precisely in the laceration caused by the contradictions.... In this way, man as image of God is thereby crucified man." Between the figure of terrestrial man, formed out of clay, whom Christ with us has assumed in the Incarnation and the glory of the Resurrection, there is to be found the cross—the path of the contradictions and the disfigurements of the image toward conformity with the Son in whom the glory of God is manifested passes through the pain of the Cross. Among the Fathers of the Church, Maximus the Confessor most reflected upon this connection between divine likeness and the Cross. Man is called to "synergy", to cooperation with God, but has placed himself in opposition to God. This opposition is "an attack on the nature of man". It "disfigures the true countenance of man, the image of God, because it detaches man from God and directs him towards himself, erecting thereby the tyranny of selfishness among men".

From within human nature itself, Christ overcame this contrast, his transformation in communion—the obedience of Jesus, his dying unto himself, becomes the true exodus that frees man from his inner fall and leads him to unity with the love of God. The Crucified thus becomes the living "icon of love". Precisely in the Crucified, in his flayed and beaten face, man once again becomes the transparency of God, the image of God that shines forth anew. In this way the light of divine love lies specifically upon suffering people, in whom the splendor of the creation has been externally dimmed. Because these people are in a special way similar to the crucified Christ, to the icon of love, they have drawn near to a special shared nature with him who alone is the image of God.

We can say of them, as Tertullian said of Christ, "However wretched his body may be ... it will always be my Christ" (*Adv. Marc.* III, 17, 2). However great their suffering may be, however disfigured or dimmed their human existence may be, they will always be the favorite children of our Lord and they will always be his image in a special way. Taking the tension between the hidden and future manifestation of the image of God as our point of departure, we can apply the words of the First Letter of John to the question we have posed: "We are God's children now; it does not yet appear what we shall be" (3:2). In all human beings—but especially in those who suffer—we love what they shall be and what in reality they already are. They are already children of God—they are in the image of Christ even though what they will become is not yet manifest.

Christ on the Cross likened himself in definitive fashion to the poorest, the most defenseless, the most abandoned, and the most despised. And among these there are those who are the topic of our discussion here today, those whose rational soul is unable to express itself perfectly because of an infirm or sick brain, as though, for one reason or another, matter were resisting being taken up by the spirit. Here Jesus reveals the essence of humanity, that which is its real fulfillment—not intelligence or beauty, and even less wealth or pleasure, but the ability to love and to consent lovingly to the will of the Father, however disconcerting this may be.

But the Passion of Jesus leads on to his Resurrection. The risen Christ is the culminating point of history, the glorious Adam toward whom the first Adam, the "terrestrial" Adam, was directed. The end of the divine project thus expresses itself: every man is on a journey between the first and second Adam. None of us is fully himself. Each one of us must become himself, like the grain of wheat that must die in order to bear forth fruit, in the same way as the risen Christ is infinitely fruitful because he has given of himself infinitely.

One of the great joys of our paradise will undoubtedly be to discover the wonders that love has worked within us and in each of our brothers and sisters—in the sickest, most unfairly treated, most afflicted, most suffering of our brethren, while we did not understand how love on their part was even possible, while their love remained hidden in the mystery of Christ.

Yes, one of our great joys will be to discover our brothers and sisters in all the splendor of their humanity, in all their splendor as images of God.

The Church believes now in this future splendor. She wants to pay great attention to this and to emphasize even the smallest sign of this splendor that can already be seen. This is because in the beyond, each of us will shine more brightly the more we have imitated Christ in the context and the opportunities we have been given.

But I would like to bear witness here to the love the Church bears toward those who suffer mentally. Yes, the Church loves you. She bears for you that natural "preference" borne by mothers for the most suffering of their children. She adopts a stance of admiration not only toward what you will be, but also toward what you are now: images of Christ.

[You are] images of Christ who should be honored, respected, helped to the utmost, certainly, but, above all, images of Christ who are bearers of an essential message about the truth of man, a message that we tend to forget too often: our value in the eyes of God does not depend upon intelligence, stability of character, or the health that enables us to engage in many actions of generosity. These elements could disappear at any moment. Our value in the eyes of God depends solely upon the choice we have taken to love as much as possible, to love as much as possible in truth.

To say that God has created us in his image means that he wanted each one of us to express an aspect of his infinite splendor, that he has a design for each of us, that each of us is destined to enter—by means of an itinerary that is specific to him—into blessed eternity.

The dignity of man is not something that presents itself visually—it is neither measurable nor quantifiable; it escapes the parameters of scientific or technological reason. But our civilization and our humanism have achieved progress only to the extent to which this dignity has been more universally and more fully bestowed upon ever greater numbers of people. Every step backward in this movement of expansion, every ideology or political action that expels certain human beings from the category of those who deserve respect, would involve a return to barbarity. And we know that, unfortunately, the threat of our barbarity always hangs over those of our brothers and sisters who suffer from a mental impediment or illness. One of our tasks as Christians is to ensure that their humanity, their dignity, and their vocation as creatures in the image and likeness of God are fully recognized, respected, and promoted.

I would like to take this opportunity that has been given to me to thank all those—and there are many engaged in thought or research, the study or promotion of different kinds of treatment—who are committed to ensuring that this image becomes ever more recognizable.

ACKNOWLEDGMENTS

I thank my editor, Nicolas Diat, for his faithfulness, his bravery, and his exactness.

Robert Cardinal Sarah